AUTHENTIC LEARNING

in the Digital Age

Engaging Students Through Inquiry

ASCD MEMBER BOOK

Many ASCD members received this book as a
member benefit upon its initial release.

Learn more at: **www.ascd.org/memberbooks**

AUTHENTIC LEARNING

in the Digital Age

Engaging Students Through Inquiry

LARISSA PAHOMOV

Alexandria, Virginia USA

1703 N. Beauregard St. • Alexandria, VA 22311-1714 USA
Phone: 800-933-2723 or 703-578-9600 • Fax: 703-575-5400
Website: www.ascd.org • E-mail: member@ascd.org
Author guidelines: www.ascd.org/write

Judy Seltz, *Executive Director*; Stefani Roth, *Publisher*; Genny Ostertag, *Director, Content Acquisitions*; Allison Scott, *Acquisitions Editor*; Julie Houtz, *Director, Book Editing & Production*; Deborah Siegel, *Editor*; Louise Bova, *Senior Graphic Designer*; Mike Kalyan, *Manager, Production Services*; Valerie Younkin, *Production Designer*; Kyle Steichen, *Production Specialist*

PAPERBACK ISBN: 978-1-4166-1956-7   ASCD product 115009

Quantity discounts: 10–49, 10%; 50+, 15%; 1,000+, special discounts (e-mail programteam@ascd.org or call 800-933-2723, ext. 5773, or 703-575-5773). Also available in e-book formats. For desk copies, go to www.ascd.org/deskcopy.

ASCD Member Book No. FY 15-2 (Nov 2014 PSI+). ASCD Member Books mail to Premium (P), Select (S), and Institutional Plus (I+) members on this schedule: Jan, PSI+; Feb, P; Apr, PSI+; May, P; Jul, PSI+; Aug, P; Sep, PSI+; Nov, PSI+; Dec, P. For current details on membership, see www.ascd.org/membership.

Library of Congress Cataloging-in-Publication Data
Pahomov, Larissa.
    Authentic learning in the digital age : engaging students through inquiry / Larissa Pahomov.
        pages cm
    Includes bibliographical references and index.
1. Inquiry-based learning. 2. Educational technology. 3. Internet in education. I. Title.
    LB1027.23.P36 2014
    371.3—dc23

                                                                    2014028827

23 22 21 20 19 18 17 16 15 14   1 2 3 4 5 6 7 8 9 10 11 12

AUTHENTIC LEARNING
in the Digital Age

Engaging Students Through Inquiry

Foreword

What happens when reality exceeds the dream you had?

This book is, in many ways, the answer to that question. In 2005, I was hired by the school district of Philadelphia to work on the school that, in September 2006, opened its doors as the Science Leadership Academy (SLA), an inquiry-driven, project-based high school formed in partnership between the school district and The Franklin Institute, Philadelphia's famous science and technology museum.

The founding ideas of Science Leadership Academy—the concept that students can ask powerful questions and create meaningful artifacts of their learning in a caring environment—are simple ones, grounded in the work of many educators who have come before us. We have worked to marry those ideas to the promise of the new technologies of our age, along with systems and structures to make it easy for anyone coming into our community—students, teachers, or parents—to ramp up to the kind of learning we value most at SLA.

That basic framework—a few powerful ideas with clear structures for implementation—paired with the truly inspiring goodwill, intelligence, and passion of the many teachers, students, and parents who took on the challenge of building a school together has created a school that matters. As principal and founder of the school, I am awed on a daily basis by the incredible work that is done by the teachers and students who make up our community. The ideas that fly around our classrooms, the amazing projects that students do, and the undeniable pride that our students take in their school all exceed the highest expectations I had any right to have back in 2005.

One of the most frequent questions I get is, "What has changed about what you believe since you started SLA?" And, interestingly, there are subtle changes in much about the way we think about all our big ideas since we started, but, if anything, I think we believe more deeply in those ideas now than we did then. Back then, we had a sense we were onto something, but, really, we had no idea how it was going to turn out. Eight years into the experiment, we find ourselves falling back on our best ideas time and time again. The ideas that asking good questions, caring about the people around us, and building structures that make it easier for people to succeed have grounded us in all the conversations we have at SLA, and, more often than not, those core concepts provide the framework that allows us to answer the new questions and challenges we face.

But simple doesn't mean easy. The work and the ideas that you will read in this book are the result of hours of collaboration and discussion and even, sometimes, arguments. The work we do, while we take a lot of pride in it, often still feels like work. There are days, like in any school—or any community really—where we get frustrated or don't feel good about what we are doing or feel like we are failing. But that is where the ethic of care really comes into play. What you will see come out in these pages is a community of learners who truly do care for one another. And when you are asking people to do the hard work of authentic, empowering learning, that care is essential. The work people at SLA do is hard. It is taxing. It is frustrating. And yes, it is exciting and awesome, too, but without a caring community to get you through the hard parts, many of us—including me—would fall short of many of our goals.

And that care doesn't end at the schoolhouse door. One of the many things that amaze me about our community at SLA is how much everyone really does believe that our school has the responsibility to share what we do with the world. Whether it is through their writing, through the work we do as Dell's Center of Excellence, or through the many conferences where SLA teachers and students facilitate meaningful conversations about education, the SLA community has taken up the mission of trying to make the world of education a better place by sharing their work and their stories. This book is a powerful representation of that task.

And in this book, Larissa Pahomov has the unenviable task of taking the work of 25 teachers and 500 students and distilling the ideas, passions, systems, and structures of the school so that other educators can learn from what we have done. Larissa is perfectly suited to the task, so much so that while working on the project, she referred to it as "the school's book," and the proceeds from its sale are going directly to SLA.

Larissa has taken the voices of our community—students, teachers, partners, and even me—and woven them together with the systems and structures and ideas we have built together to create what I hope you find to be both an immensely readable and powerfully useful book. It is not meant to be read as a proscriptive "This is the way to do school now" text—to do that would be to miss the very point of our school. Read it as a book of vision, of structures, of plans and of voices, and use it to help refine your own vision and voice of what school and learning can be.

The community of learners of SLA has taken a dream I had—that school could be better than it was—and made it greater than I had a right to imagine. Larissa has done an amazing job of wrangling that dream into a text she—and we –can be proud to share. Enjoy.

Chris Lehmann
Principal, Science Leadership Academy

1 Education for the Information Age

If you are reading this book, you are likely already committed to (or are at least interested in making the shift to) working in an inquiry-based classroom. You believe that students should be constructing knowledge instead of having teachers hand it to them. You avoid delivering lectures and like to give students some kind of choice in their assignments, favoring projects and papers over tests and quizzes. You create opportunities for students to teach and learn from each other. When you were preparing to be a teacher, you read the works of John Dewey, and you agreed with him: "'Knowledge,' in the sense of information, means the working capital, the indispensable resources, of further inquiry; of finding out, or learning, more things" (Dewey, 1916).

Almost 100 years after he published *Democracy and Education*, Dewey's words have never been truer. As the amount of information available to us explodes, as well as our access to it, what matters is not what students know but how they acquire that knowledge and what they can do with it. In terms of employment, mastering a single set of knowledge hardly helps a student. The Bureau of Labor Statistics reports that students who go to college have an average of 11.7 different jobs in a lifetime (see http://www.bls.gov/nls/nlsy79r24jobsbyedu.pdf)—and this data is based on baby boomers, who have benefited from more job security than their children. Cognitive skills such as conducting independent research, assessing information for credibility, applying concepts to new situations, and self-critiquing one's own abilities are central to our success in today's working world and, more important, to our lives as learners and human beings. In the words of education theorist Will Richardson (2012), we have begun "crafting a new narrative around learning"—one that he witnessed firsthand when his teenage son leveraged many different information sources in order to figure out how to play the video game *Minecraft*. Richardson describes the joys but also the implied perils of this narrative in his book *Why School?* (2012): "In this new story, real learning happens anywhere, anytime, with anyone we like—not just with a teacher and some same-age peers, in a classroom, from September to June. More important, it happens around things we learners choose to learn, not what someone else tells us to learn."

Unfortunately, contemporary education also harbors forces that run contrary to the tried-and-true practice of inquiry-based education. In the era of No Child Left Behind, standardized tests are the yardstick by which many schools must prove their worth, and student-generated projects are typically not accepted in place of the multiple-choice exams. The Common Core State Standards—rejected by some states for being too restrictive—also threaten to force teachers to deliver large chunks of standardized content, leaving little or no time for students to engage with what interests them personally. Administrators are often sympathetic to classroom teachers in terms of the havoc that standards can wreak on authentic learning but are rarely in a position to run interference. Teachers are left with a quandary: How can they create an authentic learning environment in today's standards-driven atmosphere?

The answer is that many of them already do—and this book will show you how. The following chapters present a detailed framework for implementing a personalized, inquiry-based education in a typical secondary classroom. The framework has five core principles, which are modeled after the scientific method and were pioneered at a real high school called the Science Leadership Academy (SLA) in Philadelphia, Pennsylvania. The word *framework* is intentional here—unlike a script or an instruction set, the examples presented in this book are designed to give educators a solid but open structure that can guide their own curriculum and classroom design. Moreover, you can use this framework to transition the content and skills you already cover, thereby providing students with a meaningful education while still meeting the educational requirements of your school, district, or state.

This book also provides detailed insight on how to effectively integrate technology into inquiry-based education. Currently, teachers and schools often fall into an embrace/reject dichotomy when it comes to using technology in the classroom. They either hop on the bandwagon with each new shiny tool, or they proclaim technology a "distraction" and ban it from their classrooms entirely. These splits often run across generational lines, and you can probably point to where the division happens in your own school building. You might even recognize such a split in yourself. Both sides of the argument have their point. But this "digital divide" often reflects a misguided focus on the *what* of technology, instead of the *why* and the *how*. The teachers who resist technology integration are, by extension, willfully ignoring ways it could change their classrooms for the better. The teachers who embrace technology sometimes miss this opportunity as well—they are excited to use a new tool, but they focus on the simple presence of that new device instead of thinking about how it could influence their curriculum or teaching. (Unfortunately this approach is reinforced by much of the education technology industry, which focuses on the latest devices and software in the interest of maximizing profit margins.)

In his book *Education Nation,* Milton Chen (2010) characterizes this kind of split as "resulting in a waste of precious time, resources, and policies, and, most of all, little impact on student learning" (p. 23). Instead of falling into an either/or debate, he urges educators to reconcile apparent opposites with a "smarter synthesis" that looks at the bigger picture of learning.

In this book, this adjustment means shifting away from looking at technology as an end in itself and toward using technology as a medium for all kinds of learning. To make that shift, schools and teachers need to be asking the following question: *How can technology transform education?*

Students can help answer this question for schools, because they are already exploring and benefiting from the transformative properties of technology as they use it outside of the classroom. As a result, students are often ahead of the game when it comes to personalizing their own learning. According to the Pew Research Center, teens have unprecedented access to tech tools. In 2012, 93 percent had a computer at home and 37 percent had their own smart phone (Madden, Lenhart, Duggan, Cortesi, & Gasser, 2013). The next section describes several of the positive effects of technology on learning, along with examples of how teens (and many adults) are already making this shift on their own time.

The Transformative Effects of Technology

In many ways, access to—and effective use of—technology involves turning the traditional methods of education on their head. The transformation extends to many aspects of teaching and learning, including what is emphasized; how students interact with teachers, other students, and people outside the classroom; and classroom management.

Shifting the emphasis from content to skills

When an education is content-based, the primary skill being practiced is memorization: you learn it, you repeat it, and you've shown mastery of the information. This process is an essential part of human learning, and being able to do it well has certain benefits. However, it only works when the memorized content will be applied on a regular basis—the Pythagorean theorem in geometry, or the lyrics of your favorite pop song that you like to sing in the shower. When we ask students to memorize content that they are never going to apply to a task, they quickly forget it. Why base education on such a rudimentary skill?

Technology shines a light on this weakness in education because it makes that basic content incredibly easy to access. Information that resided in a heavy textbook or a distant corner of the school library can now be pulled up instantly, anywhere, which undercuts the argument that "you have to memorize this now so that you know it later." When students are liberated from the monotony of memorization, they have time to learn the deeper frameworks and contexts that give facts and figures meaning. Then they can apply these understandings to *any* content they encounter in the future. The skills that they learn become the enduring understandings of their education.

Allowing for constant engagement

Along with being easy to use, technology also provides constant access to both the information and the tools needed for authentic learning. Students often have round-the-clock access to a computer, sometimes provided by their school. Where this is not the case, cell phones are becoming increasingly powerful proxies for traditional machines.

Because students so readily embrace tech tools, they are already benefiting from the power of access—doing rapid-fire research via an Internet search, mastering the skills needed to do well at an online game, or creating unique multimedia content and sharing it with the world. Consider the difficulty that teens once had in procuring the knowledge that would help them grow as learners. In the documentary *The Beatles Anthology*, Paul McCartney tells a story about the early days of playing guitar, when he and his friends were still learning basic chords. When they hear about a "bloke across town" who knows how to play a B7, they spend the day taking several buses across Liverpool just so they can learn it. The story is charming, but completely antiquated by today's standards. Musicians now can pick up all of the basic instruction they need online; a search for "B7 chord" on YouTube results in approximately 19,100 videos, the most popular of which has been viewed over 278,000 times. Constant access to resources and communities means more time to actually practice and create instead of slowly tracking down basic information.

Educators sometimes look down on these independent activities as something that distracts students from their academic pursuits. But this kind of access can also enhance education when the curriculum capitalizes on it. The research, problem-solving, and content-creation skills that students are developing on their own time can reap big rewards in the classroom, provided that time and space are allotted for such activities.

One specific aspect of this engagement is the level of connection that is suddenly possible for teachers and their students. Everyone is a part of the same online world, whether watching the same videos or being members of the same social media network. This is something of a brave new world for educators, figuring out how to navigate an online realm where they can constantly be in touch with their students and have access to each other's lives in ways that never happened when contact ended with the school day. Unfortunately, many school administrations respond to this new dynamic by attempting to restrict or ban online contact between teachers and students, when it would be more useful and instructive to model appropriate behavior and etiquette before students become adults (more on this topic in Chapter 7, "Embracing the Culture").

Democratizing learning

Technology can bring increased democracy in a variety of ways. The first, and perhaps more obvious, is curriculum-based. Because technology—and, in particular, access to the Internet—allows learning to become personalized, it allows for infinite possibilities for learning inside a single classroom. In a traditional "gatekeeper" classroom model, the teacher must impart all relevant knowledge to students personally because the teacher is the "expert" in that subject. In a classroom with integrated technology, however, access to the Internet gives students the flexibility to pursue their own personal interests. The teacher no longer has to serve as the sole source of knowledge.

Of course, this doesn't mean that the teacher has no purpose. Instead of primarily lecturing students on content, the teacher must now aid and assist students in their own quest for knowledge. This shift in focus does not happen automatically; there are plenty of classrooms where students could be exploring their own interests within a given topic but instead are still subjected to a one-size-fits-all curriculum. The shift must be intentional.

Integrated technology can also support an intentional shift toward a more democratized classroom structure. In a typical classroom setting, only one person speaks at a time, and this person is most frequently the teacher, followed by a handful of the most confident students. The same goes for written interaction; students produce papers that only the teacher reads and comments on, or they give presentations to the class but receive feedback from only the teacher. Some classrooms include small-group work, but even then, the loud voices dominate the conversation.

This one-person-at-a-time approach can be useful, but it seems outdated compared with the many different ways that students communicate with each other online. Typically they are having text-message discussions with multiple people at once, and they hop in and out of group chats or hangouts. An individual might start a conversation thread online, and then anybody who wants to comment may do so—and that conversation could go on for days, depending on how popular it becomes.

It's when students are trying to engage with all of these conversation mediums at once that teachers worry that they are multitasking themselves to distraction. However, each individual method of online communication has its value in the classroom. Student interaction can be both highly synchronous, with everybody commenting at once, or highly asynchronous, with student work being archived for later observation or use. It is important to note that the teacher's voice, when filtered through technology, does not automatically have more weight; suddenly the teacher is just another commenter on the discussion thread, or another face in the video chat. This reality certainly requires a shift in thinking on the part of educators, but the increase in student voice makes the transition worthwhile.

Connecting to "the real world"

The previous sections of this chapter have discussed the benefits of students having access to contemporary, relevant materials. Many teachers already make space for this in their classroom by bringing in the latest bestselling novel or a news article relevant to the current unit. Technology makes it easier to bring in the outside world, but doing so is not impossible without it.

Where technology does provide a tremendous shift, however, is in making it simple for students to reach out to that larger world. Instead of just observing what takes place beyond the school walls, students can now contribute to current movements, debates, and initiatives. On a basic level, this access makes it much easier for students to participate in some of the more traditional ways of "speaking up" in society. For example, students can submit letters to the editor electronically or approach politicians via social media. These methods can provide an increased sense of confidence and legitimacy that speaking up in person cannot (on the Internet, nobody knows you're a teenager).

Of course, this kind of traditional communication is only a small piece of what can be accomplished via technology in the classroom. The assignment that gets handed in to the teacher and is never seen by anybody else may not feel like real work, whereas the project that has to be polished for public consumption via an online portfolio is as real as it gets. By leveraging the Internet as a showcase space, especially by plugging into existing venues for written and multimedia work, students experience the pride of being "professional" and get the benefit of outside feedback.

Just as they navigate student-teacher relationships online, schools are also tasked with the challenge of dealing with how their students present both the best and worst versions of themselves on the Internet. Students may be savvy in the methods of online communication, but they can also be blissfully ignorant as to who has access to whatever they share. Again, teachers do students a disservice when they seek to limit or ignore their connection to the online world. It will happen no matter what, and it will be messier without involvement and guidance from adults.

Simplifying the back-end work

Many schools still print and sell paper agenda books, but the most organized students (and teachers!) have eschewed these planners in favor of online calendars and to-do lists, with reminders and organizers built in.

Teachers can benefit from this transition not only for their own lives, but also for the management of their classrooms. When materials can be distributed via an online hub, there's no more making copies and taking time to hand them out in class (as well as no chance that the students can lose the paper). When grades can be updated electronically and accessed directly by students, they can review progress reports at their own pace and on their own schedule, as well as benefit from programs that help them analyze their strengths and weaknesses within their own performance. Technology can even greatly alleviate the stress of providing feedback; most teachers can type faster than they can handwrite, and when they finish their commentary, they can send it right back to students instead of letting it languish in a folder.

These all may seem like technical points, but it's important for teachers to recognize the transformative value of technology for their own practice, not just for their students. Curiously, this is often the last area where teachers make a change, even though it provides them with the most immediate benefit. The first year I worked at SLA, I made my students print out their essays so that I could comment on them by hand. The second year, I did the same thing. The third year, I finally realized there were a dozen ways I could facilitate that process online, and I haven't looked back.

A New Framework for Learning

When technology is meaningfully integrated into an inquiry-based classroom, the classroom benefits from the positive transformations just described. Unfortunately, these transformations do not happen automatically when a classroom gets a set of laptops. If teachers or schools want to, they can use technology to prop up the same old curriculum and policies. (A multiple-choice exam given on a laptop is still just a multiple-choice exam.) Usually this lack of transformation is due to a lack of enthusiasm for innovation on the part of the educators. Sometimes, however, technology can enable the worst qualities of our educational system. The possibilities for surveillance of students via their devices, for example, is downright frightening and has already led to a lawsuit in Pennsylvania (Kravets, 2010).

If the meaningful use of technology democratizes a classroom, then the guide to making that shift cannot be authoritarian or prescriptive. Instead of a rigid set of rules for implementation, classrooms need a framework that is solid in its approach toward teaching and learning but leaves room for educators to adapt technology to their subject area and teaching style. This kind of framework both maximizes the transformative properties of technology and minimizes its potential misuse.

The founding teachers of SLA set out to create this kind of framework before their school opened its doors in the fall of 2006. They spent the summer considering the environment they wished to create, and what conditions would need to be established. This effort included figuring out how to successfully maximize the use of technology, since the school would have a one-to-one laptop program for all students. Although the teachers knew that they would be working with some very new classroom protocols, their inspiration for the framework of the school came from an older, more established source: the scientific method. This choice led to the school's development of its core values.

The five core values

Five core values serve as the anchor for teaching and learning at SLA, and serve as the outline for this book

- **Inquiry**—Authentic learning can happen only when there is a legitimate desire to gain knowledge or skills. Students need to be able to ask their own questions (with varying degrees of guidance) in order to engage with their education.
- **Research**—In a world where our access to information is becoming limitless, what matters is no longer how much you already know, but how well you can find what you need to know. Students need to learn how to both collect and interpret their own data, as well as identify and assess outside sources for quality and credibility.

- **Collaboration**—Whether in person or electronically, collaboration has become a cornerstone of the work life of adults, yet students are typically expected to produce and prove their knowledge in isolation. Working together not only supports students in their pursuit of personal achievement; it also helps them develop interpersonal skills that are essential for their future professional lives.
- **Presentation**—This skill is often pigeonholed as the "front of the room" presentation that students loathe. Presentation is actually a skill that students use constantly, both in the classroom and, increasingly, online. Bad presentation skills can be damaging to both their professional and personal reputations, so knowing how to present themselves and their work appropriately and effectively is essential.
- **Reflection**—How do we improve ourselves? Curriculum is often written as a race to the finish line, without any time or space for students to consider what they could do differently, or better. Reflection provides a necessary pause between presenting a finished work and beginning a new line of inquiry, and helps ensure that students (and teachers) improve with each cycle of learning.

Success of the model

The SLA was founded at a time when students and families in Philadelphia were looking for learning environments that improved upon the traditional high school model, and the school has proven itself a place that can produce conventional success through progressive methods. The school's project-based model has also proven no barrier to achievement on standardized tests. In 2012, more than 80 percent of students scored proficient or higher on state exams in both reading and math, with a less than 5 percent gap between white and black students. And after nine years, the school has seen five classes to graduation with a 99 percent graduation rate; 98 percent of those students go on to college—with close to $4 million in scholarship money awarded to graduates in 2013.

What matters more, of course, is how students benefit from their education after they've graduated. We actually warn students that they are likely to be surprised (and possibly uninspired) by their freshman lecture-hall courses in college; but graduates quickly discover that their writing, reading, and research skills are more advanced than those of most of their new peers. "You taught me how to think" is a common refrain when students come back to visit the school—as they frequently do, during holiday breaks or on a random day when they're not in class. The level of connection that graduates still feel to their high school is remarkable. The school was, simply put, somewhere they wanted to be. Just as adults enjoy a work environment that engages and challenges them, students will respond to a school that values their individual contribution to their learning.

How This Book Is Organized

Each of the next five chapters describes a core value in detail, with the following features:

- **Introduction**—A detailed breakdown of how this concept can transform your classroom practice, with a discussion of "the digital connection" for each of these qualities.
- **A Framework for the Classroom**—A point-by-point list of directives for implementing this core value in your teaching, with specific examples from real teachers and their curriculum. At the end of each section, there's also a "Making the Shift" feature that presents the first two steps you can take to bring this practice into your classroom.
- **Student Perspectives**—Brief, insightful anecdotes from SLA graduates about their experiences mastering the core values and how a value has helped them after high school.
- **Roadblocks and Work-arounds**—Advice based on the experience of teachers who have implemented these values and already know the most common challenges. This section provides solutions in advance, helping you avoid these roadblocks before they appear.

- **Schoolwide Practices**—Tips and tricks for expanding the use of this value beyond an individual classroom.

At the end of the book, a chapter titled "Embracing the Culture" describes some of the larger policies and protocols in place that can help facilitate authentic learning schoolwide.

How to Use This Book and How It Can Help You

Like any comprehensive education text, this book can be both read cover-to-cover and also returned to as a reference. Hopefully the text will provide you with so many useful suggestions and examples that you will do some extensive highlighting and note-taking! This framework can be adopted by an individual teacher, a group of cooperating teachers, an entire school or a whole district; it can be used to overhaul a curriculum during the summer or used for instruction ideas in the middle of the school year. At SLA, the framework is universal, but its design allows individual teachers at the school to bring their personal touch to the curriculum they design while staying true to the five core values. The next chapters provide multiple examples of their application of the framework, and additional resources appear in the appendices.

Most important is the fact that although the framework was developed at a school that has a one-to-one student laptop program, *you do not need this level of access to technology in order to adopt the core values described in this book.* The framework does not rely on any particular brand of device, software, or app, and although the examples include plenty of references to students using electronic devices, much of what the students do can be emulated offline.

As discussed earlier in this chapter, educators are often stuck in a false dichotomy of being either for or against the use of technology. This book can help you circumvent that debate by providing you with a model of how to use technology *meaningfully*, to support a personalized-inquiry curriculum. This process will likely affirm some of the pedagogical methods you already believe in. It will also probably sneak in some new ideas you hadn't considered before—and you'll be pleasantly surprised at the results with your students.

That is not to say that this transformation is easy or without its challenges. As with any framework, there are a few common pitfalls that educators are likely to run up against. Smaller ones are addressed in the "roadblocks" section of each chapter, but here are a few overarching pieces of advice.

Make time and space for the practice

At SLA, the challenge of making time and space for inquiry-based, personalized teaching and learning is often framed with the question "where does it live?" Over the course of your own education and career, you have likely encountered great new ideas or methods, resolved to try them out, and then watched the entire school year zip by without finding a sliver of time to implement what you know would really be a good thing for your students. Even when you do manage to set aside a time for the new approach, the results often aren't as effective as you had hoped.

Adopting a model of personalized inquiry can do wonders in your classroom, but as with any new approach, students need set-up and modeling for it to stick. If adopting this framework means a change in how you run your classroom, let students know that they are in for something different, and make sure you provide ample and explicit instruction as you go through new modes of instruction and assessment. (If the powers that be won't allow for an entire year of this style of curriculum, make the shift for the last part of the year instead of the first. It will be hard to get kids to go back to a more traditional classroom setting after they've enjoyed the empowerment and autonomy of personalized inquiry.)

Make room for student inquiry

Once the time and space have been made, the next step is making sure that students' authentic impulses as learners are honored. In a traditional curriculum, inquiry is frequently labeled as being off-topic—if all of the content to be learned is already set, then anything else that students bring up can only be tangential. This kind of narrow track needs to be traded for personalized courses of study that students (mostly) pilot themselves. This approach can certainly involve some instruction that is more traditional, but that instruction is always presented with the intention of preparing students to learn on their own instead of preparing for a factual exam.

Don't forget to provide support

The inverse of the previous problem is that instead of stifling student inquiry, teachers give students so much room that the class loses focus. Although this model is very much student-driven, it is still meant to be school. This is part of why this book is not called *Individualized Learning*; in the education technology industry, the term *individualized* often connotes an entirely automated learning program, with no teacher present. In the model presented in this book, students are not meant to be left completely to their own devices (literally and figuratively). They may develop their own line of inquiry, but they will need your feedback in refining their questions. They may collect their own data sources, but they will need your guidance with interpreting statistics and determining credibility. You will be learning along with the students, and your status as a learning expert will provide them with the support they need so that their work is the best it can be.

CR

I hope that you find these next chapters both challenging and helpful—that they help your thinking in terms of your teaching practice but also provide you with ample support and examples to make that challenge a reality. As teachers, we must set the tone for our students by engaging ourselves in the "further inquiry" that Dewey described all those years ago. This book is a roadmap for that process.

STUDENT PERSPECTIVE: LIFE AFTER SLA

Jenn Wright, Class of 2013

Before I came to SLA, I thrived at a traditional Catholic middle school. I was the bookworm in my class, that annoying peer who struggled to stay in her seat as she raised her hand for each and every question. I liked school because it came naturally to me—simple as that. I also cared deeply about the difference between a 97 percent and a 98 percent, and, to be honest, I equated a lot of my self-worth to the gap between those two numbers.

Learning through projects at SLA was a huge transition for me, and that was challenging at the beginning because it was the first time I was partially responsible for another person's grade and someone else for mine. I learned the importance of investing into the questions being posed. I figured out how knowing your own strengths and weaknesses helps to understand those of others to more effectively work together. I learned to take ownership of the quality of my work because it was being judged by my peers through in-class presentations and the general public via the Internet.

Fast-forward to college, where my peers once again care quite deeply about the disparity between an *A-* and an *A*. I'm relearning how my grade depends upon just four assessments, two papers, and two exams, and most of the people around me only care to know that they are above the class average and curve.

I manage to distance myself from a grade-obsessed mindset because I now understand how to put learning into context. Learning in a project-based curriculum showed me how the knowledge in a particular field builds and is not meant to stop once the last chapter of the textbook comes and goes. I put stock into the connections I am able to make on my own between the material in the classes I take and the world around me, as well as the relationships I develop with my professors—the people who are actually observing the trends and developing the material I am learning.

2 | Constructing Inquiry

"Why is the world the way that it is?"

This question is probably as broad as it gets. There's certainly no right or wrong response. It is the kind of question that can inspire lengthy debates based on deeply held beliefs, but it is also the driving force behind research into the many different aspects of human existence. Naturally, it's un-Googleable. A search gives you results but no real answers.

This question is also the basis for 11th grade analytical writing at SLA. On the second or third day of class, students are presented with the question in English class and informed that this is their task until June—to tackle that question, however they interpret it, repeatedly over the school year, and to turn their responses into a series of two-page essays. This portfolio-style assignment, called the "2Fer" essays, is a cornerstone of the 11th grade curriculum. Both beloved and feared by the student body, it removes the single biggest barrier (or safety net, depending on how students feel) from authentic student inquiry. Starting now, *I'm not going to tell you what to write about.*

Of course, the introduction of that single question about the world isn't the end of our conversation about the assignment. Nor is it where student-centered inquiry begins at SLA. Students already have two years of this kind of learning under their belt, and teachers have been purposefully scaffolding a "zoom out" process in which we have, in fact, been telling students what to write about, only in increasingly less specific terms with each passing semester. The 2Fer essay assignment may seem revolutionary compared to your traditional English essay prompt, likc throwing students into the deep end, but it's actually a carefully placed step in the process of constructing student inquiry.

At its simplest, the practice of inquiry is the practice of asking a question. However, to define inquiry as just "asking questions" is too reductive. It's also the way that teachers can trick themselves into believing that they're facilitating inquiry in their classrooms. Letting students ask deep questions is nice, but those questions alone do not transform a curriculum. Real transformation requires a plan.

Characteristics of Authentic Inquiry-Based Instruction

Asking questions is just the tip of the iceberg. What happens when students are allowed to follow their queries into the deep? For inquiry to be successful, students need to have the space to identify, explore, and resolve the questions and problems that motivate them to learn. For this to happen in the classroom, the teacher must allow the following three values to become central into their instruction: *choice*, *personalization*, and *relevance*. Embracing these values in the curriculum also leads to an increase of *empowerment* and *care* for both teachers and students. These five characteristics of authentic inquiry-based education—as it is defined by SLA principal Chris Lehmann—are described in detail in the next sections.

Choice

The right to make choices is an inexorable part of a free society. From apples in the supermarket to candidates in an election, we believe that freedom of choice is not only a good thing, but also that it's necessary for both our personal fulfillment and a functioning world.

By contrast, schools are some of the most rigid, choice-free environments where humans have to spend time. Everybody is supposed to be in an exact place at an exact time, learning (or, in some cases, teaching) an exact thing, and if you're not doing what you're supposed to be doing, you're probably going to get "written up." Students might be offered a few options, but they are often tightly hemmed in by exterior requirements placed on their education ("You don't have to take math *and* science senior year, but you have to take at least one to graduate.") or instructions that are more prescriptive than supportive ("Your essay was great, but you lost points for going above the page limit."). Curriculum is often based on covering a certain amount of content, and getting in this "coverage" often pushes out time for real inquiry ("I'd love to spend more time exploring the themes of this chapter, but we have to prepare for the test on Friday.").

Compare these scenarios to those in some of the professions that we value most in society. They all make choices that involve some risk, but the ability to make independent decisions is central to their success. The president of the United States must carefully weigh what matters most to the nation and then chart a course of action that reflects those priorities, in addition to dealing with the urgent affairs that cross his desk. He is aided by a staff of hundreds who give their lives to the work, and even then they cover only a fraction of what they set out to do. Research scientists and university professors do not organize projects that repeat what has already been done—they are hoping to advance, and even revolutionize, their fields of study. As a result, their project timelines often change, and sometimes the focus shifts several times before the end is in sight. Architects and engineers are challenged to improve our quality of life with their designs, and the most lauded are those who succeed in thinking outside the box and making an innovative choice.

This is not to say that structure is useless. Indeed, each of the professions described are also subject to—and often benefit from—external guidelines and constraints placed on their work. But their *best* work is not a direct result of these structures. Good structure gives them the freedom to choose a course of action that will produce the best result, whether that's a life-saving vaccine or a new method of construction. By contrast, jobs that allow *no* choice—flipping burgers, picking avocados, working an assembly line—are not seen as desirable by society, and with good reason. Because there's little or no inquiry involved in these tasks, they're often mind-numbingly boring.

The same holds true for education. A traditional sequence of courses has its value, as do logistical structures such as set class times and students changing rooms. Inquiry can thrive in these settings. The danger comes when teachers force the learning itself to be as regimented as the school day and the academic calendar—each task at its appointed time and place, with identical outcomes for each student.

I suspect that most adults can recount a classroom experience that bored them because of a lack of inquiry. I have a particularly painful memory of a 4th grade math class wherein the teacher lectured us on the concepts behind fractions by cutting a page of construction paper into progressively smaller sections—and then had each student produce identical posters, labeled just like her sample on the board. Unfortunately, many students are treated like this all the time—as though they wouldn't learn anything if they had the freedom to direct their own learning. By contrast, trusting students to make at least some of their own choices about what they learn fosters student investment and engagement, promoting deep understanding of content and, ultimately, retention of these individual, self-selected inquiry experiences.

➤ **The digital connection.** Before access to technology became common in schools, classrooms were often barren of resources. At best, the classroom had a small library or maybe an encyclopedia, but the most common resource—a set of textbooks—hardly allowed for students to pick and choose. Teachers who wanted to support inquiry had to go beyond the norm, arranging for a subscription to a newspaper or scheduling a visit to the library. When choice was allowed, it was very much a planned, intentional act, usually for a major assignment. It was not a part of the daily routine.

Contrast that with today, when most students can access the world's information from a device they keep in their pocket. Choice takes very little effort and can now be incorporated into the classroom on a micro level. Want students to explore averages? Have them pull up the current statistics of their favorite sports team. Need them to learn about poetic form? Everybody gets to pick a writer that speaks to them. Choice doesn't mean that students choose *everything*; it means that the curriculum respects that they have preferences, and honors those preferences as much as it can.

Personalization

Of course, allowing students to make a choice can't simply be a theoretical practice ("Those are all great ideas about how to solve this problem. Now I'm going to show you the right way to do it."). Once they have selected a line of inquiry, students must also be allowed to pursue it to its natural conclusion.

This approach draws the classroom even further away from a standardized curriculum model. Not only are students having their own individual thoughts, but they're actually doing their own individual work, as well—often during class time. Compared to the vision of the traditional classroom, this scene looks like chaos. But thinking back to the different examples of work in the previous section, this model is how much of the world works. Think of staff offices in the West Wing of the White House, or the deconstructed working space of a tech start-up, or even a financial trading floor. These organizations trust individuals to conceive of complex tasks and complete them individually, without prescriptive instructions or constant oversight. Students may not yet be working at the same caliber as these professionals, but practicing the metacognitive skills of this kind of work is just as important as gaining the content knowledge relevant to their field of interest.

➤ **The digital connection.** This is one area where the presence of digital tools can really transform the learning environment. In a traditional setting, students are heavily reliant on the teacher to disseminate the knowledge and skills that they need to complete any task assigned. Teachers are naturally positioned as the masters of their subject, with the students residing on a lower plane. This hierarchy is effectively turned on its head when students can look up anything they want on the Internet. For power-hungry teachers, nothing is more threatening than a question that they don't know the answer to; but for personalized inquiry, teachers must not only accept but embrace the fact that students no longer have to direct every question they have toward the "expert" in the room.

This approach, of course, does not require access to the Internet. ("You don't know what that word means? Me neither. Let's get out the dictionary.") The beauty of having access to a knowledge base as vast and speedy as the World Wide Web, however, is that it quickly dispenses with more superficial lines of inquiry. When students can quickly access basic content such as maps, timelines, databases, and formulas, as well as tutorials and models for relevant skills, they can then devote more of their energy toward the deeper questions that drive the need for those resources. Moreover, the personal line of inquiry is what motivates them to gather all of that information in the first place.

When played out to the extreme, this vision of personalized education can remove the teacher from the picture entirely. If students can access everything they need on their own via the Internet, the thinking goes, why not just have that be their primary resource for learning? This method is already gaining traction, with decentralized efforts like user-generated video tutorials on YouTube, and also more structured programs such as Khan Academy. Methods like these for self-directed learning are valuable, and they are also how many professionals further their education once they are out of a traditional learning environment. However, the practice of this isolated, "individualized" learning does not accurately reflect the way that most people work. A good boss guides employees to the best resources and environments for their tasks; likewise, a good teacher aids students in their personalized quest for knowledge. This might involve redirecting students when they've selected an untrustworthy resource or asking a question to clarify their line of inquiry. In any case, teachers are no longer the master of the classroom; teachers are positioned alongside the students, helping each one pursue what matters to them.

Relevance

We've all heard the refrain "Why do we need to learn this?" If we didn't have all the inquiry drummed out of us in school, hopefully we were asking the same thing when we were students. How did your teachers react? Did they attempt an answer, and did you buy what they were selling? The desire for relevance is a powerful one, and students are quick to notice when no effort is made to justify the curriculum that is being served to them.

Inquiry makes learning relevant because there is a basic assumption embedded into the practice: What do *you* want to know? That question automatically honors the value of the student's personal perspective and experience. When students respond, they are taking ownership of their own learning. And when the inquiry is so embedded that students are producing their own questions, nobody asks "why" of the curriculum because the "why" *is* the curriculum.

➤ **The digital connection.** Again, digital tools can transform learning by bringing a new level of relevance to the previously cloistered classroom. The traditional textbook—a stand-in for the power-hungry teacher as a gatekeeper of knowledge—draws rigid boundaries around what a student can potentially learn. (If it's not in the index, forget about it.) By contrast, students have access to unlimited, up-to-date information on the Internet. This resource is certainly messier than a survey textbook, but learning to evaluate sources is a part of the process. (You'll find more on this topic in Chapter 3, "Facilitating Research.")

It's important to remember that *relevant* does not have to mean "cutting edge" or even "contemporary." Many core bodies of knowledge that have been around since ancient times are still central to student learning. The key is giving the students the autonomy to gain access to these bodies of knowledge while they are pursuing lines of inquiry that feel relevant to them personally.

Empowerment

Alongside an absence of choice, schools are intentionally designed to deny students control. In a typical high school, students are expected to absorb six or seven different subjects each day, which includes meeting the expectations of six or seven instructors, each with a certain set of course instructions, grading systems, classroom rules, and pet peeves. Everybody will spend the same amount of time on each section of content, and the entire class is expected to achieve the same amount of learning by the end of the year—and they will all demonstrate their understanding through an identical medium, such as a test or an essay.

How did education become such a cookie-cutter enterprise? The simple answer is that it's the most efficient approach. Students can't all be indulged with a private tutor, so the lessons must be deliverable to a large group. And student achievement needs to be assessed, so the curriculum must be standardized as well.

The sinister side to these seemingly innocent rationales is that they place no faith in the individual ability of students. At best, the result produces a population of people who are very good at taking orders. This leads to an efficient workforce. If you include basic technology education, students then become the "21st century workforce."

Politicians often give lip service to this as the end goal of education, which is sadly incomplete. In an inquiry-based education, students do more than learn how to follow instructions to use the latest tools well. When students are encouraged to ask "why" and "how" of their world, they also begin to want to effect positive change in their environment. The inquiry process encourages them to become educated citizens who have the confidence to take action when necessary.

➤ **The digital connection.** Students' fluency with digital tools elevates their voice in society—they can design websites, produce videos, and manage social media with a savvy that often outshines that of the adults doing the same work. When students are supported in exploring problems and issues that matter to them, they will leverage these skills to educate and instigate positive change—creating an online petition to stop budget cuts to their school, or making a video PSA to address teen violence. Many examples of this kind of work can be found online at the Student Voice website: http://www.stuvoice .org.

Care

The last item on this list is something of a hidden characteristic in an inquiry-based curriculum. Care is not always explicitly discussed, and yet student learning would not be successful without it. A pitfall of the current focus on standards-based instruction and high-stakes testing is that individuality is marginalized. This is not to say that benchmarks, learning targets, or standards don't provide useful structure for instruction and assessment, but rather that a by-product of this focus on test scores to measure "success" is a reduction of students to percentiles and statistics. Students are shuffled from grade to grade with little concern for personal mastery, and when their personal achievement *is* measured, we use deficit-focused terms such as *failure* and *remediation* to define their struggle.

By contrast, personalized learning in an inquiry-based classroom takes place in a caring environment that fosters individual growth and isn't based on measuring one student against another. Each of the other four elements—giving students choice, allowing them to personalize their learning, embracing what is relevant to them, and encouraging their empowerment—respects and honors the students. Care shines through naturally. This approach in turn fosters students' intrinsic motivation and promotes student engagement in learning because it is relevant to them, ultimately empowering students as life-long learners. In this vibrant learning environment, the content and skills defined in standards can be acquired without alienating students or reducing them to letter grades and test scores.

A Framework for Classroom Inquiry

Part of the joy of an inquiry-based curriculum is that each teacher is facilitating a unique path toward knowledge through a common framework. The components of that framework are the following:

- Identify the essential questions for learning.
- Identify what students need to learn—and then what is variable.
- Build a flexible framework for assessment.
- Model inquiry on a daily basis.

The next sections elaborate on each of these components and provide tips on how to begin making the shift toward this approach.

Identify the essential questions for learning

On a superficial level, identifying the essential questions for learning means developing some kind of "hook" that will engage students when the material is introduced. In inquiry-based education, it means identifying meaningful lines of inquiry that thread through the entire unit and show students the core value of exploring this particular topic. This concept is nothing new. In the Understanding by Design (UbD) curriculum framework developed by Grant Wiggins and Jay McTighe, "essential questions" are a necessary cornerstone of lesson planning. These questions should be open-ended, without a specific factual answer, such as "What makes a plant alive?" instead of "What are the stages of photosynthesis?" These open-ended questions lead to more inquiry, thereby driving the unit. The essential-question process also reflects six facets of understanding, each one increasingly complex:

Explanation: What keeps a rollercoaster from flying off the tracks?

Interpretation: What are the symbolic meaning(s) of *Guernica* by Pablo Picasso?

Application: How can the law of sines and cosines be used to measure the natural world?

Perspective: What did Union and Confederate soldiers think of the Civil War and its aftermath?

Empathy: Can you relate to the villain Iago in Shakespeare's "Othello?"

Self-knowledge: What did you gain from this project, including where you struggled or failed?

The best essential questions reach for the more challenging facets. (For a thorough description of how to write essential questions, consult the books written by Wiggins and McTighe, especially *Essential Questions: Opening Doors to Student Understanding.*)

Getting students to create their own quality questions is not an instant process, but you can achieve success faster than you might think. Science teacher Gamal Sherif succeeds in this endeavor with his freshmen via a curriculum that leaves space for students to explore what they really want to know. At the beginning of their biochemistry course, these threads of inquiry come out more informally on top of the set course of study. During a study of proteins, for example, students are asked to go "above and beyond" by synthesizing and making new connections from the basic facts. After students describe how proteins are made at a cellular level, they then enrich their comprehension by describing biological diseases or mutations that can result from too many or too few proteins. "The students are really interested in disease and mutation. That interest helps make traditional protein synthesis so much more meaningful," explains Sherif.

Several months later, during the dissection project, students are asked to record at the beginning: "What do we want to learn?" Then they shift into creating a project that reflects their particular interest in classification. "We basically started out with some prompts from the teacher regarding the anatomical similarities and differences between species," Sherif says. "From there, students moved into questions about how the anatomies were alike or different in a much wider range of species (other than human or grasshopper). Students then designed an investigation (lab- and web-based) to learn more about their questions." Here are some of the inquiry write-ups that students have produced in previous years:

> To further our learning, we dissected a grasshopper and a frog. We dissected so that we can compare the anatomies of all the organisms. Our hypothesis was that the ratio between the body size and the body system size would be the same.

> With our first animal, the grasshopper, we had difficulty finding organs and completing the dissection itself, therefore we reviewed and re-conducted the experiment. After the second dissection of the grasshopper we finally had some good questions. For example, since we were conscientious of the environment, we wanted to know how these species were treated before they were dissected.

> In our observations, we found that every species we studied had similar organs and functions. A question that we had was if the behavior of the animals were similar to each other while they were alive.

Writing good essential questions is often seen as a master's task, but Sherif's approach shows that, with healthy parameters and thorough scaffolding, students who are new to this kind of learning can also develop their own lines of inquiry.

MAKING THE SHIFT

1. Think back: When you studied this subject area yourself, what captured you about the content? Saying "I was always a _____ person" doesn't count. Figure out what ideas, conflicts, idiosyncrasies, or practices specifically attracted you to exploring this subject. Do those essential, attractive features shine through in your curriculum?

2. Think ahead: What role does this subject play in today's world? In what way does the knowledge gained help students explore, analyze, criticize, or solve a current problem or issue? When they're out in the "real world," how will they be expected to apply this knowledge? Have them participate in that task now, instead of waiting until they've become adults.

Identify what students need to learn— and then what is variable

In a given subject, standards or benchmarks—and potentially state curriculum—define what skills and content students must master. Within a given curriculum map, the trick is to identify where students will have the freedom to construct inquiry on their own. If the goal of an activity is acquisition of content knowledge, perhaps you can vary the presentation method. For example, students could have a checklist of information about a particular historical era and then choose a specific medium for sharing those facts with the general public—essay, slideshow, podcast, video, and exhibit being just a few of the options. Alternately, if the goal is skill mastery, students can apply the specified skill to problems and situations that they select on their own, such as applying the same mathematical formulas to analyze statistical data on a topic or field of their choice, be it professional sports or neighborhood crime. The most advanced students can be offered control over both content and methods—what's important to learn, and how to present it.

For his anatomy and physiology class, science teacher Tim Best built a few clever variables into how his students demonstrated their knowledge. Best knew that he needed to balance leaving room for student inquiry with ensuring that students gained a working knowledge of the systems of the body—without making rote memorization the cornerstone of the course, which is the typical approach to studying medicine. The result of his work is an elegant set of units that walk through the 10 systems of the body while also tracking the physiological phases of human life. A particularly popular project among students is the first one, which asks students to follow their "specimen"—from fertilization to 10 years old—and then make a scrapbook of its development, including its manufactured medical issues. The students are provided with a detailed checklist of the knowledge they need to demonstrate, as well as a list of portfolio "scenarios" that they must include in their final scrapbooks ("In Utero Development" and "Playground Accident" are two notable ones). Students have freedom in how they respond to these scenarios and must also write additional ones, checking off the learning objectives that pertain to the systems they've selected to study. At the end of the unit, the class has a set of highly individualized scrapbooks, as well as a working knowledge of the skeletal, nervous, and digestive systems.

By contrast, English and history teacher Joshua Block's "Crossing Boundaries" project has sophomores master a common skill and then get very personal with it. The class learns the methods of creating a successful interview podcast—listening to professional examples, identifying interesting topics and subjects, conducting interviews, and editing and producing the final product. These skills are explicitly modeled and practiced in class, from listening to and deconstructing episodes of the radio program *This American Life* to participating in mock interviews. The only prompt that students are given for the content of their podcast, however, is the phrase "crossing boundaries," which provides them with a meaningful focus without limiting their topic selection. Students have explored the stories that define them and those close to them, from immigrant tales to gender transition to questions of faith and religion. The project gives them the skills to make meaning out of the experiences that define us as humans.

MAKING THE SHIFT

1. Make a list: What is the essential knowledge students need to master in your class? Do this activity "blind," without looking at your curriculum or lesson plans. When you think your list is complete, compare this to what you currently teach. This activity is designed not to make you throw out lessons, but to figure out what specific, nonessential content could be made variable. The particular experiment, poem, historical era, or application that you find fascinating might bore your students. Get ready to give them the chance to make their own choices there.

2. Brainstorm: What are all the different ways that a student could display an enduring understanding of those essential pieces of knowledge? These ideas are the seeds of personalized learning. Try to make a list for each item, and when you are finished, look for any themes or patterns. These could become the basic criteria for an inquiry-based project.

Build a flexible framework for assessment

If either the content or the skills (or both) are variable, students will need a means of assessment and feedback that is flexible without being vague. For the most personalized inquiry-based projects, this can mean that students write their own checklists and rubrics for what mastery looks like. In most cases, though, it is the teacher's responsibility to communicate which pieces of learning are essential in the unit, with specific examples and models of how students can demonstrate they have mastered the material. In Tim Best's anatomy and physiology project, for example, he provides students with a 23-point checklist of bodily functions that they must demonstrate in their final scrapbooks, with instructions as detailed as "Describe the events that lead to the generation of a nerve impulse and its conduction from one neuron to another." This helps students keep track of the small details in the midst of project creation, which can get messy at times. Best also breaks the benchmark down into four smaller deadlines, with students completing a couple of portfolio scenarios at a time before the final scrapbook is due. In addition to keeping students on track, this approach gives him a natural time to check in on their progress.

Checklists and check-ins help students keep the details in order, but rubrics are what provide them with meaningful feedback about whether their project exceeds, meets, approaches, or does not meet expectations. The categories for assessment can vary depending on the subject, although SLA uses a set that can be applied to any topic: design, knowledge, application, presentation, and process (see the sample rubric in Appendix A). The teacher must visualize what a successful project looks like, and then describe what success looks like in each category—but that description does not include a laundry list of content. Best's rubric, for example, simply states that the "scrapbook demonstrates factual knowledge of the digestive, skeletal and nervous systems." How that knowledge is demonstrated is left to the student. Best assesses the project while sitting next to the student, seeing how many of the 23 points the student has hit, and then turns that into a point value for the "knowledge" category of the rubric. (Rubrics and feedback are discussed more in Chapter 6, "Making Reflection Relevant.")

MAKING THE SHIFT

1. Identify criteria: From the previous brainstorm, explore the list of ways that students could demonstrate enduring understanding. Often the basic criteria for an inquiry-based project are embedded in that list; this can be the basis of your write-up and rubric.

> **MAKING THE SHIFT**—*(continued)*
>
> **2. Establish norms:** Consider the time and energy that students can reasonably be expected to devote to this project, and create clear guidelines that reflect that expectation. The guidelines can include specifics like page length, time limits for a presentation or video, and intermediate deadlines. Removing the guesswork lets students focus their inquiry on the actual content of the project, not its requirements.

Model inquiry on a daily basis

Inquiry-based education does not preclude direct instruction or even tests and quizzes. Sometimes those approaches are the fastest path to knowledge acquisition. But in an authentic inquiry-based classroom, students need to know that what they are learning will help them answer the deeper questions that have already been posed or that they are generating as the unit continues. Moreover, as described in the "Choice" section of this chapter, you can easily incorporate inquiry on a micro level by building activities that allow students to plug in material that is relevant to them personally.

Many traditional activities can be subtly shifted toward being inquiry-based with a minor change in emphasis. English teacher Matt Kay, for example, relies on thoughtful questions for his students' warm-up journals, constantly loops back to the essential questions of a unit during class discussions, and has a few writing prompts that he uses repeatedly throughout the year, such as "What would this character be doing right now?"

"You want to make them OK with the idea that they're reaching toward something that they're not going to get—but also ensure that they're not feeling frustrated by that," Kay says of the process. "It's a puzzle that they never quite fix."

MAKING THE SHIFT

1. Analyze: What are the key questions that your class activities seek to answer? These might be the essential questions of the unit, or they might be a simple query about what methods are best for mastering a particular skill; but every task should seek to answer some unknown. Make these questions clear to students by sharing them frequently and displaying them in the room whenever possible.

2. Establish norms: Have your students ever heard you say, "I don't know the answer to that"? Reinforce the idea that inquiry is the natural state of humankind. Look at the class activities that force a path on students, and see if they can be reworked to let students find their own way. Provide the time and space to do it well, and be an active participant in the process yourself. When you give instructions, instead of saying "Do you have any questions?" ask them instead, "What questions do you have?"

Roadblocks and Work-arounds

Teacher: "How do I plan for something as unpredictable as inquiry?" The outcome of an inquiry-based unit may be unpredictable, but do not assume this means it was poorly planned. The most detailed, rigid planning needs to go into the core of the unit, especially with regard to the essential questions. By contrast, the day-to-day planning needs to reflect that the course of those lessons may be determined by student inquiry. This doesn't mean that class can't be carefully scheduled or organized; the activities just need to support the pursuit of inquiry, whether it's an open-ended discussion or direct instruction to give students the tools they need for their own work.

This also means, of course, that teachers can't rush in and fix the puzzle when things start to get messy. For inquiry to work, teachers can't have the answer in their head. If they do, the discussion is not inquiry-based; it's just a version of what I like to call "guess what's in the teacher's brain." The fail-safe way to avoid this is to have students construct their own questions.

Of course, all teachers ask *some* questions that they know the answer to, as a way to check for basic understanding. Kay's freshman English class, for example, often starts with "what happened" in a book, either through a quick summary or maybe a recollection quiz. But these moments are not the centerpiece of instruction; they are only in the superficial levels of the UbD's six facets of understanding mentioned earlier (explanation, interpretation, application, perspective, empathy, and self-knowledge). The essential questions are what help students move beyond the "what" of a text; the questions draw the discussion deeper, into themes that will carry across the unit and build enduring understandings for students instead of just check for basic comprehension.

Teacher: "How do we make time for inquiry while still covering the content we need to?" The supposed conflict between inquiry and content coverage can be quickly diffused with some structure from the teacher. Inquiry should not have to be a free-for-all; directing students toward particular bodies of knowledge is totally acceptable (and they often appreciate the guidance). Best's anatomy project design, for example, had an explicit and lengthy list of concepts to be covered. However, the project did not attempt to approximate the endless memorization that characterizes the study of science, and anatomy in particular. Best doesn't love giving his students a 23-point checklist, but that list actually condenses the hundreds of objectives in the anatomy textbook that he consulted while designing the project. "Details can be looked up and relearned," he says of the core science knowledge. "The important thing is that our students are learning how to think, learn, solve problems, ask questions, and find the answers to these questions."

A true inquiry-based curriculum knows that content is not the paramount goal of student learning. The goal is to make students life-long learners, capable of acquiring any knowledge they need, when they need it. Take a second look at your list of what your class "needs to get to." What on that list will they forget in a week anyway? The reality of standardized testing means that some content may need to be covered in a particular way, at a particular time—but once it's over, move on.

Student: "I don't know what to make/what to write about." When a person has limited choices, nothing seems more exciting than freedom. But once that freedom is granted, the variety of choices available can quickly become overwhelming. This feeling can also come from a place of apathy; students soon discover that picking their own line of inquiry takes more work than just having a topic handed to them.

Providing some kind of parameter for the work helps avoid this situation, whether it's a finite list of topics or a set of activities in which the variety comes from the topics you choose. This kind of structure doesn't impede inquiry; it advances it.

For inquiry that is more open-ended, help students reach for ideas that are close to them. When it's time for my students to write essays prompted by the question "Why is the world the way that it is?" I remind them that the terms "the world" or "society" should never be in their thesis statement; otherwise they'll end up writing a book, not a two-page paper. For students who are really stuck, I guide them toward content that they've encountered recently. What's the last TV show or commercial they watched? What was the message of this program, and what methods were used to get it across? Look for the relevant spark in students' lives, while reminding them that it does not have to come from a topic that is traditionally regarded as "important." Sometimes that spark comes from challenging the very notion of inquiry-based education. I would often suggest to the most frustrated students that they analyze the shortcomings of the very assignment they were writing about. "Writing a 2Fer about a 2Fer" became the ultimate challenge in the class. In most cases, students get over their visceral negativity and actually make some good points, which in turn helps me improve the project design.

Student: "Somebody already had this idea." Another common pitfall of inquiry-based education is that once students are given open access to "the real world," they discover how much has already been thought of, researched, and analyzed by somebody else. At first they're inspired by the research they've discovered, but then they despair when they realize that the science fair project they thought was clever and unique has actually been done hundreds of times. Their ideas feel insignificant by comparison.

Overall, this experience is a positive one for students; it encourages both humility and a desire to go beyond their first good idea. However, a preoccupation with originality can quickly derail the process of inquiry-based learning. To advance past this roadblock, remind students that the world is large, and that it's not a bad thing for similar ideas to develop independently of each other. For the 2Fer essay assignments, the guideline for thesis statements is that they should be "unique, insightful, and debatable"—with the caveat that "unique" simply means that the statement reflects their own thought process, not that their idea has never been expressed before in the history of mankind. If the work will be a valuable learning experience, it doesn't matter that the idea has already been explored. If their focus still feels too close to something already out there, encourage them to extract the core of their idea and apply it to a different situation. If that bacterial growth project has been thoroughly explored with yogurt, what other foodstuffs would be interesting to test? If that critical theory has been thoroughly applied to the classics of literature, how about applying it to last summer's blockbusters?

Another way around this roadblock is to have students "zoom out" and analyze the history of a situation or an idea instead of simply taking sides on a well-trod issue. For many of the great debates of humanity—whether it's about the existence of a god, the morality of the death penalty, or the value of nuclear power—the sides have been thoroughly explored and have even become entrenched. These are topics that really *have* been argued to death on the Internet, but how did these disagreements develop into what they are today? What do these situations say about our current culture, our values and prejudices, or human nature? This approach is particularly useful in humanities classes, where rhetoric has the habit of trumping logic.

Modeling Inquiry Schoolwide

SLA teachers use the UbD framework to design their courses, but the concept of "essential questions" is integrated into all levels of the school and its structures. The school itself has three guiding questions:

- *How do we learn?*
- *What can we create?*
- *What does it mean to lead?*

In addition, the school developed gradewide themes for the freshman, sophomore, and junior years. These themes are interdisciplinary and are explicitly addressed in English, history, and science classes. They also build on each other from year to year. The freshman theme, for example, is "Identity" and is encapsulated in these questions:

- *Who am I?*
- *How do I interact with the environment?*
- *How does the environment affect me?*

In the next year, students are asked to build on the discoveries they have made via these questions with the sophomore theme of "Systems":

- *How are systems created and defined?*
- *How do systems shape the world?*
- *What is the role of the individual in systems?*

Junior year capitalizes on the advancing skills and capacities of the student body with the more proactive theme of "Change":

- *What causes individual and systemic change?*
- *What is the role of the individual in creating and sustaining change?*
- *What is the relationship between the self and the changing world?*

For senior year, the yearlong theme is "Creation," and no essential questions are provided. Students follow a more individualized course of study and are expected to take charge of identifying their own lines of inquiry in class.

These yearlong themes were first brainstormed by the founding teachers, before the school even opened, and the wording of each set of questions was fine-tuned as each grade came into being. Although neither the themes nor the questions have been changed since then, they're not set in stone, and the teachers are committed to them in part because they know they can be updated if necessary. The questions are meant to be integral to planning as well as instruction, and they grace the top of each UbD unit plan that teachers produce (when I write my own plans, I have a habit of putting the one or two questions that unit addresses in bold). The gradewide essential questions are also posted prominently in classrooms. Although students may not be able to recall the exact wording of the questions, they readily remember key projects related to each theme. Good inquiry-based curriculum design ensures that the essential questions lead to relevant, enduring understanding.

Although this kind of schoolwide support certainly helps to create a culture of inquiry, these methods can also be used within an individual department, or even a single classroom. Whatever the boundaries of implementation, the important thing is consistency within those boundaries. If students are going to be empowered to inquire, then that power should be handed to them as completely as possible, given the constraints of the environment.

Back to the Beginning

This chapter started with a broad question: "Why is the world the way that it is?" It's a hook that leads to some great thinking and discussion. It shows students just how big their inquiry can be.

But this big-picture, philosophical discussion quickly gets narrowed down. I immediately follow up with a template version of the question: "Why is _____ the way that it is?" With photographs as prompts, we talk through a couple of topics that can be inserted: government, a traditional classroom, a refrigerator. Then I make the second part of the question variable as well: "the way that it is" needs to be replaced with specific, measurable criteria. Suddenly we've gone from vague ruminations about the nature of the world to focused questions such as "Why are high schools so focused on grades and rankings?" Classroom inquiry needs this kind of guiding framework in order to turn student wonder into active learning.

All this is to say that, for this framework to be successful, inquiry must be at the center. It cannot be relegated to the annual research project, or the last five minutes of class, or after students have completed the traditional test. Everything that students do must be justified by a relevant question or problem posed.

STUDENT PERSPECTIVE: CAPSTONE PROJECT

Abe Musselman, Class of 2013

For my senior capstone project, I created a textbook for students who were trying out the guitar for the first time. The beginning steps were easy enough; I drew up a couple diagrams on MS Paint and wrote about a hundred guitar TABs of my favorite songs, working harder than I had since completing my college applications. The lessons portion presented a different challenge, though. I wanted to cover all the basics of technique and theory, but I also had a feeling that there was more to it than just the instruction.

I thought back to the first time I picked up a guitar. I had been inspired by the way my favorite musicians were able to reach into this swirling cloud of notes and chords and pull out something tangible, something with shape and form. That's what drove me to spend hours on end practicing Travis songs, picking and searching for the best fuzz pedals. I knew I could eventually understand how it all worked and, even more exciting, I was in charge.

Memories of my own early learning showed me the solution. The best way I could help kids learn the guitar was to make them want to look for answers on their own. I started by citing some resources that I regularly turn to for great music, quality discussion, and expert help. I wanted kids to throw themselves headlong into the world of guitar, not just to learn "Wonder-wall" and move on. I also included sections about my favorite guitarists and some of the incredible things they were able to accomplish. By the end, I was satisfied that my project would get readers to that crucial first step of asking questions, and that I provided enough instructional text to answer them. It was more than just information, it was the experience of appreciating the enormity of everything you don't already know and realizing you can find it out if you ask the right questions.

3 Facilitating Research

When SLA teacher Matthew VanKouwenberg teaches his freshman biochemistry course, he starts the year off with something fun: building paper airplanes.

The practice of starting a course with a collaborative activity is nothing new; it helps students get to know each other and allows them to dive into the hands-on learning right away, instead of getting bogged down in course policies and procedures. VanKouwenberg's activity, however, serves an additional purpose of introducing basic research methods. Each group must produce one paper-plane prototype and then send it flying a total of five times, keeping a record of the distances reached via measurements taped on the floor. When the plane has made its final landing, students must then discuss and decide: How could they make two changes to the design to make their altered design plane go farther? Once they reach a consensus, they build a second prototype and send it flying again. After this round, they assess their altered design and then must *undo* one of the two changes they made, in the hope that this will actually extend the length of the flight.

The paper plane activity embodies several of the core values of the school's framework, with research at the center. Students engage in this essential piece of the scientific method without even realizing it. That the activity uses a playful, freewheeling activity as its medium is by design. We've all fashioned paper airplanes at some point in our lives, and some of us have probably even discovered the perfect fold. But did it ever occur to us to use a formalized system of trial and error?

This activity involves no "book research." In fact, it's one of the few times that VanKouwenberg actually discourages students from "looking it up," seeing as the web is full of tutorials on how to build a better paper airplane. Working in slightly artificial conditions, the students can't just consult an outside source and call it a day. Through their hands-on research, they themselves must become the experts in their chosen field. The research must be thoughtful if they are going to benefit from it, and that means that all of their methods must be sound—from the initial directions to the final analysis.

This kind of research is commonplace among professionals. Adults are expected to independently explore and extrapolate the information that will help them do better work. At the high school level, however, "research" is often defined as turning to and then quoting the experts, be it in history, literature, science, or another subject area. These skills are valuable, but they represent only one piece of the research methods puzzle. Students need to be aware of the many ways in which they can research the world around them, and that includes through their own design.

Factors That Support Student Research

To aid students in the process of research design, teachers must facilitate research that allows for *autonomy*, *activity*, and *metacognition*. The following sections elaborate on each of these qualities.

Autonomy

Just as students should be allowed at least some choice in developing their line of inquiry for a project, so too should they be allowed to explore the wide world of content available to them as potential resources. Instead of being limited to the boundaries of an encyclopedia or a textbook, what topic will lead them to content that interests them personally? This approach has the added bonus of keeping research fresh. If students aren't hemmed in by a particular source or a predetermined list, they might hit on a topic that has yet to be studied or analyzed. Perhaps they have a relative with an uncommon disease, or they love an artist whose work has not yet been popularized, or they live in a neighborhood whose history is undocumented. Their work could make a relevant contribution to our collective knowledge.

➤ **The digital connection.** If students are given the freedom to explore topics beyond the traditional boundaries of their discipline, they will also need to know how to identify, access, and interpret information. This means getting them to think about where those current resources might live—not in a textbook or an online journal, but closer to whoever the "experts" in their topic are. SLA starts its students on this shift in thinking during their Summer Institute for incoming freshmen. Each "expedition group" is given a different section of the city to visit and develop a line of inquiry about. As group members determine what might interest their peers for the closing presentation, they dig into the current resources online—museum and monument websites, civic and business organizations, local news sources, and historic preservation groups. None of this content has been collected and analyzed by professional researchers for the purpose of education, which is precisely what makes the students' work so meaningful. (More on Summer Institute in Chapter 7, "Embracing the Culture.")

Activity

The level of engagement in student research can be assessed on a spectrum. "Passive" research is what happens when the information has already been processed and provided to students. Most textbooks are on this end of the spectrum, with information and concepts neatly summarized for students, sometimes without any illustrative examples of where this information came from. Note that sometimes this summary can be useful—students shouldn't have to seek out the original source of a mathematical formula or track down the birth certificate of a famous individual to find out when he or she was born. The same is true for many secondary resources, which are key in understanding how the critical thought around a discipline has developed. The point is that the information is essential, and students shouldn't have to work hard to find it.

Next on the spectrum are resources "in the rough." Where these fall on the spectrum depends on whether the content has already been deemed relevant and who has singlcd that content out, both of which affect how easily the source can be accessed. Primary sources that are considered important by a large number of people are easy to access, whereas more specialized information pertinent to a smaller group of people may be more difficult to find. For example, nobody has to travel to the National Archives in Washington, D.C., to read the Declaration of Independence—and that's a good thing. On the other hand, if students are looking into the relationship between insects and agriculture in their county, they will have to work harder to find relevant sources of information. Students' level of activity depends on how deep they are digging. The more specific they get, the more they will have to work to seek out the right kind of collection or repository for their research.

Students really get "active" with their research when they begin to seek out this kind of uncollected content. This can include information that has not yet been packaged for general consumption, such as raw statistical data, personal journals and letters, unedited video and audio footage, or critical commentary that has not appeared in the mainstream media. Sometimes the information being presented is relevant to their field of study; sometimes it is not. All of this means more work for the students—but also a greater chance that they will uncover something unique, possibly revelatory.

Finally, on the far end of the "active" side of the spectrum lies research that generates its own content. Here students can absolutely expect that they will uncover something unique, because they will be collecting new data. Of course, the themes and conclusions they come to may resemble ideas already put forth by established researchers; but working with unique content ensures that those discoveries will also be authentic to the student. Science labs are the most obvious example of this practice, as they typically require students to personally observe and measure some aspect of the natural world. Equally valuable are methods of social research such as surveys, personal interviews, and case studies.

Active research requires the greatest amount of skill but also promises the greatest possible rewards. Students should use the passive types of research to support these more independent endeavors, not the other way around.

➤ **The digital connection.** Many resources for passive research are easier to access online than they are via print—think search engine versus scouring the bookshelf or an index. Students are likely to discover websites that they will turn to multiple times. To keep the searching at a minimum, students should keep a compendium of these sources handy. A class list can be created, with the first items provided by the teacher. In contrast to the automatic authority entrusted to a textbook, engaging students with this kind of research requires a more detailed discussion of the criteria used to determine credibility. Students must be coached to consider who authored and published each piece and what that person's bias might be in presenting the information. (More on determining credibility later in this chapter.)

For active research, digital tools are essential when it's time to manage data collection. Anybody who's ever tried to transcribe an interview while it's happening knows that an audio recorder does wonders for the process. The same is true for video, automated tables for statistics, and devices with GPS capability. Computers can handle massive amounts of this kind of data, but tablets and smartphones can easily capture it as well. Taking the grunt work out of active research frees students to collect more information and thereby have a larger pool of data on which to base their conclusions.

Metacognition

In passive, more traditional research, students are expected to direct their attention outward, in order to evaluate potential sources as they encounter them. Once students are engaged in active research, however, the quality of their data is directly influenced by the quality of their methods. As a result, they need to be looking inward as well as outward, evaluating their process before, during, and after their research activity. Collecting your own data can be something of a balancing act—if the findings do not match your hypothesis, is this because your original idea was misguided? Or is it because you're not collecting the right information? Or, alternately, are you just not analyzing from the correct angle? These questions are commonplace in a science setting but should be central to *any* research setting.

➤ **The digital connection.** Digital tools can expedite the meta-cognitive process by allowing students to quickly review the data they have collected. Are the measurements following the trend proposed by the hypothesis? Are subjects responding to the interview prompts in a meaningful way? How many hours of recording should be collected, and how far along are students toward reaching that goal? By making these quantitative assessments instant, computers allow students to spend their time on the qualitative judgments only they can make.

As described here, the research that takes place in schools has many variations. The framework that follows is designed to help teachers facilitate research of all kinds—and especially to help teachers shift toward more active, meaningful research on the part of their students.

A Framework for Classroom Research

The framework for research can be synthesized in four statements:

- Let it be personal.
- Anticipate resources that students will need, and allow access to them.
- Learn active research methods.
- Evaluate content, sources, *and* methods.

The next sections describe each of these in detail.

Let it be personal

The best research topics should feel relevant to the students researching them. This helps motivate them to do the work that will help resolve their line of inquiry. The most obvious way to facilitate relevance is by letting students choose the material they will be working with. English teacher Alexa Dunn embodies this approach with her "You and the World" project for freshmen. Subtitled "Passion, Interest,

Information, and Change," the project asks students to select a current event or contemporary issue that interests them personally and then track the ongoing evolution of that issue via both mainstream sources and their own research. When it came time for a particular group of students to collect information, "research was multifaceted and went beyond the typical," Dunn says of the process. In addition to using online and print resources, her class had to identify and connect with experts in their field, whether that was an officer from Amnesty International, the founders of an animal shelter, or their neighborhood community group. Students also had to research the venue where they wanted to complete the "change" phase of the project by making a positive impact on their issue. All of this material was reported out via a series of blog posts and, eventually, an in-school presentation.

History teacher Pearl Jonas also takes this personal approach but adds a geographic parameter by asking her students to research their immediate environment. In the 11th grade, her American history students evaluate the status of the American dream in a Philadelphia neighborhood of their choice. In recent years, their research methods included personal interviews, collecting hyper-local statistics related to housing, jobs, crime, and education, and going to community meetings. Leading up to the project, the entire class also participated in some more traditional, unified research by analyzing primary source documents about the evolution of the American dream since the 1600s. From that common base of knowledge, they were then able to compare and contrast the general model of the "dream" with the neighborhood they researched. The project covered both active and passive research methods and gave students a reason to be invested. "This project generated more excitement from my students than any other project that year," Jonas says. "My students were excited to look more deeply into their communities."

Keep in mind that research does *not* have to be self-selected in order to feel personal. The world is rich with potential venues for research, and unexpected topics can inspire students. Physics teacher Rosalind Echols drew inspiration for a project about objects in motion from a seemingly mundane experience: the morning commute. Students are asked to observe what happens on the different forms of transit they take to school. The class then uses these observations and their resulting questions to investigate the nature of physical force. Students are first surprised and then intrigued by this topic. "Most of our students ride public transportation to and from school every day," Echols says, "but many are oblivious to what is happening around them prior to doing this project." The project transforms a common experience into a site for research.

MAKING THE SHIFT

1. Make a list: Identify all of the research that your students already complete in your class. This could be anything from a comprehensive research project to simple tasks like looking up vocabulary in the dictionary. Then assess: How could these moments of research be made more personally relevant to students? Especially when the purpose of the assignment is to practice research skills instead of to master particular content, where might freedom of choice transform their engagement with the curriculum?

2. Brainstorm: What experiences or knowledge do students already have that could serve as venues for research? Keep in mind that you do not have a complete picture of what students know or what they are interested in, and your project design should leave space for that (instead of providing them with a preselected list of what you *think* will make it personal.) For a list of sample inquiry prompts, see Appendix D.

Anticipate resources that students will need, and allow access to them

For high school research that is more traditional, teachers can often anticipate and provide all of the materials that students will need for their projects. When students all focus on a particular era of history, for example, or must all write about the same book, the range of sources needed might fit on one classroom bookshelf.

Once students have the agency to pick exactly what they want to research, the print resources in your own classroom or school library aren't likely to be sufficient. Even teachers who want their students to have the freedom to choose their own subjects may feel overwhelmed by the idea of supporting so many different lines of inquiry. It's true that the students will be on their own to a greater degree than they—and you—are accustomed to. However, you can put in place a few structures to guide students toward smart research and to prevent the process from turning into a free-for-all.

For both the wealth of resources available and the speed at which they can be accessed, the Internet is a great boon for class-room research. However, this accessibility doesn't mean that students should just do random searches (remember, a good line of inquiry is un-Googleable). Setting parameters for inquiry—for example, asking students to pick a relevant article from a local news source or providing a vetted list of tutorials about lab procedure—honors student ownership of learning while still keeping instruction moving. For sources that students will use frequently, it's worthwhile to create a list of links that students can access and also contribute to (see Appendix E for examples).

Another way to anticipate resources is to brainstorm what topics students may wish to pursue. For her "American Dream" project, Pearl Jonas required "specific research elements" as a part of the final product and then provided a list: socioeconomic data, crime data, jobs available, civic organizations, green space, education opportunities, infrastructure, transportation, voting trends, and food access. This list was not exhaustive, and many students explored other aspects of their community, but creating the list gave Jonas a head start on connecting students with relevant content (and had the added bonus of providing prompts for students who weren't sure what angle to take in their neighborhood research).

For this process to work, students will need to have access to the Internet in whatever way is available to them: computer labs, class-room sets of laptops or tablets, or "bring your own device" policies. Of course, this means that students have to be trusted to actually use the Internet in class. Digital tools, including smartphones, will have to be embraced instead of banned. If this requirement is a major shift in thinking for you, keep in mind that "embrace" does not mean "use all the time." Just as students should be guided toward useful resources on the Internet, they should also be guided in their tech use via classroom norms for when and how devices can be used.

MAKING THE SHIFT

1. Brainstorm: What are your sources for knowledge on the subject you teach? What key texts, journals, databases, and websites do you rely on? Which scholars and sources do you trust? Share this list with your students, with an emphasis on the resources that you use to stay current. Make those resources as accessible as possible; if they're printed texts, keep them in the room; if they're online sources, share the links.

2. Establish norms: Create a policy for the use of technology that empowers students to treat their electronic devices as tools, not distractions (see Appendix B for an example). Instead of policing phone use, model when using your device is and isn't appropriate. Prepare to be pleasantly surprised when students start to conduct research on the fly.

Learn active research methods

By the time they reach the upper grades, students are typically proficient in the methods of more "passive" research conducted in the classroom—picking a source, reading it, taking notes, and connecting relevant content back to their thesis. However, their practice of active research methods has often been limited to the science lab, if that. Teachers who want students to collect their own data need to spend time on modeling and practicing the many different ways that students may engage with researching the world.

This process is most natural when it is integrated into the project early on. For Roz Echols's physics project about public transportation, the active research begins before students even really know the parameters of the project, and it doesn't take any extra time out of their day: "The project begins with simply asking students to observe what is happening on their commute and bring in those observations," Echols says. Students take mental notes on the bus or train to school, and then report what they noticed in class. The resulting questions jump-start the process of researching the physics of public transportation. Once they're deeper into the project, students begin to apply the equations and concepts relevant to the material, but first they have to just feel the bumps and brakes of their commutes.

For projects in which students are evaluating an experience, the research can be a natural extension of what they do every day. For projects in which students are looking into a particular subject, though, they may need a variety of tools to successfully unearth the content that will be most relevant to their work. For Pearl Jonas's "American Dream" project, students' methods varied as much as their topics. Some of them interviewed community members. Others tracked down hyper-local statistics on topics ranging from housing to employment to education. Still others integrated themselves into the structure of the neighborhood they were researching, attending community meetings and other local events. Jonas facilitated this variety of approaches by introducing students to the variety of repositories of information that students could access, including localized and "raw" sources of statistics. She also connected them with experts in these resources, such as police department employees and professional researchers.

Jonas assigned the "American Dream" project to high school juniors, who have a bit more confidence and skill when it comes to engaging with adults. Younger students can complete active research as well; it may just need to be modeled more explicitly. For her "You and the World" project with freshmen, Alexa Dunn places an extra emphasis on survey and interview skills. Many students interviewed one or two experts on their topic or assessed public opinion by creating an online survey and distributing it to the school community. The process was highly collaborative, with students turning to each other for help with fine-tuning survey and interview language, as well as clarifying what kind of data they were looking for. The project also included a component called "agent of change," in which students had to go out into the field and get involved with the issue they had researched. To do this, they practiced some of the most basic skills available to them: conducting personal visits, making phone calls, and writing e-mails.

Dunn acknowledges that active, independent research takes time and that teachers need to "front-load what that looks like" so students don't get lost in the middle of their research. Providing models from both professional and student sources helps students grasp what their own process should look like. Advice from groups like the Poynter Institute on how to prepare for an interview (http://www.poynter .org/how-tos/newsgathering-storytelling/chip-on-your-shoulder /205518/how-journalists-can-become-better-interviewers/) and what kinds of questions to ask (http://www.poynter.org/how-tos /newsgathering-storytelling/131491/6-quetions-that-can-help-journalists-find-a-focus-tell-better-stories/) can make a world of difference before students strike out on their own.

MAKING THE SHIFT

1. Identify: What active research skills might your students need to complete this project successfully? Introduce students early on to the notion of surveys and statistics, personal interviews, and field studies. The earlier in the year that they can begin practicing these skills, the more proficient they will be with each new project.

2. Model: Provide students with professional examples of this kind of research alongside samples of successful student work. For interpersonal methods such as interviews, give them time to develop their questions in workshops and to practice their skills on each other in mock sessions.

Evaluate content, sources, and methods

When students transition toward more active research, how they assess their research must shift as well. Ideally, students are already learning how to scrutinize scholarly sources—both the findings and the research methods used to determine those findings. (Theoretically, this kind of critical eye should also be applied to textbooks, whose content is sometimes accepted by students as being infallible.) However, true inquiry-based research pushes this scrutiny to the next level, because students have to evaluate their *own* research and methods as they complete the work.

As discussed earlier in this chapter, teachers can point students toward credible online resources in order to expedite the research process. Doing so can save all parties time and effort. However, a downside to this approach is that it glosses over a skill crucial to living in the digital world: assessing the credibility of information posted on the web. Mastering this skill isn't just useful for school; it prepares students for a growing, and increasingly complex, aspect of modern life.

Math teachers Erin Garvey and Brad Latimer kept this point in mind when designing their personal finance project. The assignment asks students to pick a scenario—representing either savings or credit—and to determine what the best financial plan would be. The provided scenarios often resemble situations in students' actual lives; after choosing one, they are required to write a second personalized scenario on their own. Here's an example of a provided scenario:

> You are 16 years old, and you have a part time job. You have managed to save $1,000 over the past couple of years, and you currently make $200 per month (after taxes). You want to start saving for college, as you know that books/tuition/other expenses will be significant costs. If you can afford to invest 60% of your monthly income, how should you invest your money to maximize your funds for college?

The students must research five different possibilities each for saving and credit, decide which option they think is best, and then justify their rationale in a paper. This whole project basically sends students down the rabbit hole of online personal finance, exploring the myriad of options available, and learning to evaluate the offers made by banks and credit card companies. Garvey and Latimer set the general parameters of the research—banks, credit cards, and loans—but they choose not to prescreen the sites within those categories. As a result, students must evaluate both the quality of the content ("Is this a good offer? What's the small print?") and, by extension, the credibility of the sources ("Can this company be trusted? Are their promises misleading? What is their history?") As a result, students get to struggle with the same confusing financial deals that dupe adults—but in a setting that doesn't threaten their life savings. Once the project is completed, many of the students are thrilled with their newfound expertise, and Garvey and Latimer have received reports of students going home to find better savings and credit deals for their own family's finances.

This transition from teacher-selected resources to student-selected resources does not have to happen immediately. Teachers who have provided more guidance about sources in the past can slowly remove those parameters as they see students become more comfortable with evaluating sources—or as the teachers become more comfortable with the idea themselves. Spanish teacher Mark Bey made the shift when he realized that his students could find sources for quality vocabulary as well as he could—and that the process of finding those sources would enrich their own experience of learning the language.

In his original lesson plans, Bey provided all of the necessary new vocabulary to complete a particular unit. Students had clear parameters, but the result was cookie-cutter, with projects that looked similar at the end. "I felt like I was giving the same project over and over again," Bey says of his old approach. Now, when students begin working on a new topic, he provides them with a uniform foundation of vocabulary that covers the basics, and then they must do additional research to find the terms that work for them. For a unit on fashion, for example, he gives students words such as "pants" and "shirt," but they must personalize those terms by looking up relevant adjectives, plus any items of clothing that aren't on the original list. Students do most of this research offline, using print dictionaries, to emphasize a vital habit in language learning.

This new approach embraces the exciting, and also messy, process of language acquisition. Memorizing a new word is one thing;

applying it correctly is another. To keep students on track, Bey provides instruction about syntax and sentence structure, and he actually discourages students from looking up new verbs, because learning conjugation is a separate process. And he also checks in with students as they do their research, so that he can redirect them if necessary. Many of the pointers about quality sources come from the students, and Bey simply facilitates this exchange. "We do a share-out in class— 'What things have you found that you think are good?' By the time I've checked in with the whole class, I can point them toward resources that other students are using."

In all of these examples, the expectation that students will make errors and have to redirect their approach is built into the curriculum. If teachers do not anticipate this possibility, they may see student mistakes as something that slows down the learning. With inquiry-based education, however, making mistakes is an integral part of the learning—just as it is a part of most professional work. Roz Echols's evolving attitude about student research reflects this approach: "In 'real' science, people often make mistakes in their experiments or process, or misinterpret their data.... Over the years, I have become more comfortable with this reality, and letting my students experience scientific 'research' more authentically." If students experience their learning in a vacuum, they may master the content presented, but they will not have experienced authentic practice of the methods they need to gather knowledge in the real world.

MAKING THE SHIFT

Brainstorm: Walk yourself through the research process that you want your students to undertake. Do your best to assume their mindset. Where are the challenge spots, or possible moments of confusion? Anticipate these moments so that you can provide students with the appropriate support when they need it. (Keep in mind, too, that you should not be able to anticipate every challenge they may encounter. If you can, then it's probably not an authentic research project.)

MAKING THE SHIFT—*(continued)*

Evaluate: Now that you've considered the possible challenges, go through your list and decide: Which of these moments would help educate students about the research process? Which of these moments would just derail them? This evaluation will help you set parameters for how far the students can go before they have gotten off track. Be prepared to also make these evaluations on the spot as students are working through their ideas in class.

Roadblocks and Work-arounds

Teacher: "With students exploring so many different topics, how do I watch for plagiarism?" It's true that giving students freedom in their research means that there's no way teachers can be familiar with all of the content or even the basic knowledge required for each topic. However, to assume that teachers could "manage" students and their research in order to prevent plagiarism is absurd. At some point students have to be let loose and trusted to represent their sources faithfully. For this to work, students need to be thoroughly educated on plagiarism.

There are two stages to this process. The first is to make sure that students have a working knowledge of what plagiarism actually *is*. This may sound silly to older teachers, but in the age of song sampling, Internet memes, and movie mash-ups on YouTube, the idea of proper citation and giving credit to your sources is unknown to many teens. Students may have been told that copying their friend's homework is wrong, but they also need to be introduced to the deeper academic norms that colleges expect of both their faculty and students. Most institutions of higher learning have a section of their website devoted to academic integrity, along with specific guidelines for students and descriptions of the harsh penalties imposed if students are caught cheating. Introducing these resources to students will help them understand that plagiarism is a serious offense that could jeopardize their academic futures—and it will make their current schoolwork all the more real. Once students have been introduced to the reasons behind these policies, they need to be held accountable to a consistent policy with clear consequences. (See Appendix C for SLA's school-wide Academic Integrity Policy.)

Teacher: "Students are researching, but they're lazy about it. They just grab the first sources they see." The great strength of Internet research can also be its weakness: it's instant, but it's instant. If students can have something that's "good enough" right away, then why would they spend extra time going farther afield?

To avoid this trap, students need the tools to search smarter. Searching a scholarly database does not actually take longer than a typical Internet search, especially when you factor in the time saved by not having to sort through endless unfiltered results. Replace the "I just Googled it" mindset by introducing students to the online research databases available to them. If your school is fortunate enough to have a librarian, have that person instruct the students in how to access these tools. Many public libraries also provide access to such data-bases, so getting a library card might need to be a homework assign-ment if a field trip is out of the question. Many large library systems have also produced how-to pages or even video tutorials about how to access their scholarly materials remotely. And even the ubiquitous Google search can be improved by using the Google News or Google Scholar filters. The latter will provide results from a variety of journal databases all at once (although students sometimes will run across the problem of having access only to abstracts and not the full articles).

It is also important to model research as a dynamic process, not just an easy list of do's and don'ts. The Wikipedia debate is a fine example of this. Many teachers rail against the resource and ban the site outright in their classrooms; but according to the Pew research project on Internet use in schools, 87 percent of teachers use Wikipe-dia themselves (Purcell, Heaps, Buchanan, & Friedrich, 2013). As the project put it, when it comes to online search options, teachers are "confident in their own ability to use these tools effectively," and this confidence needs to be passed along to students. Instead of forbid-ding knowledge that might be faulty, teachers need to show students how to assess whether a source can be trusted. Wikipedia makes this process easy, as entries lacking sufficient references are flagged at the top of the page for potential misinformation. If students choose to use Wikipedia or another crowd-sourced website as a baseline for knowledge, they should be checking out the "References" citation list at the bottom of each entry; those sources might lead them to resources that they could eventually use in their own work. And if the page lacks thorough citations, it should be looked at critically—just like student work without quotes from other sources.

To help see the hidden influences on their research, students also need a crash course in how Internet search engines work. Algorithms, predictive search fields, and user histories all need to be exposed and explored. Discussion of these electronic biases can serve as a launching pad for discussion about our own assumptions and blind spots when it comes to research. The *International Business Times* has a good primer on the weaknesses of Google Search (http://www.ibtimes.com/top-5-weaknesses-google-search-705927), and *Tech Republic* has an accessible explanation of how Google tracks user histories (http://www.techrepublic.com/blog/it-security/why-is-my-internet-different-from-your-internet/).

Student: "I'm finding lots of information on the topic, but I don't get it." This problem is the inverse of the previous scenario, but it produces a similar outcome. Instead of students settling for material that is simplistic or unrelated to their topic, they discover content that might be quite relevant but is more sophisticated or complex than what they are used to.

When students are all following their own research paths, classroom management can definitely get messy. If students don't recognize that this material is really beyond their grasp, they may struggle unnecessarily and shut down. Conversely, if they seek assistance, the teacher may get pulled into giving a crash course in calculus derivatives, middle English, or whatever other base knowledge the student needs for understanding.

For teachers who are used to more control in their classrooms, this may sound like a logistical headache. However, this situation also embodies one of the best aspects of authentic learning. Many classrooms don't make any space for students to reach for anything independently. Students' level of engagement should be celebrated, not undercut. Give them a heads-up in advance, letting them know that if a source leaves them flummoxed, they should do a spot check with you to see whether the material is worth pursuing. And when students do have to abandon some of the sources they've discovered, emphasize that this content is a preview of what they could eventually achieve on their own if they pursue an extended course of study in the topic. Someday students may be publishing their own mathematical proofs or ethnographic studies for the world to explore. (For that matter, the active research they complete now may also be relevant to the "real world" beyond their school. More on that in Chapter 5, "Perfecting Presentation.")

Modeling Research Schoolwide

Research is a time-consuming, discursive process, and the more accepting a school is of that fact, the more successful student research will be. This collective state of mind asks for flexibility on the part of teachers, as well as some explicit planning and modeling.

Just as an academic department plans which content will be covered at each grade level, research skills can be developed via a specific scope and sequence. In their standards for each discipline, SLA teachers have written expectations for research that build on themselves for each year of curriculum completed. The research standards for English, for example, are as follows:

- Grade 9: Student can look at a source and identify relevant material.
- Grade 10: Student can evaluate the quality of sources and identify relevant material.
- Grade 11: Student can use an independent line of inquiry to evaluate the quality of sources and identify relevant material.
- Grade 12: Student can use an independent line of inquiry to design and implement a complete research process.

The research standards for science split the development of research skills into two levels:

- Grade 9: Student can distinguish between different research methods, scientific principles, and appropriate uses of lab equipment.
- Grade 10: Student can gather and discuss meaningful data and information using multiple sources of information.

Students are assessed on whether they are approaching, meeting, or exceeding these expectations. The standards also serve as a useful touchstone for writing curriculum. Even if you didn't teach those students at the previous level, you know what research skills they were expected to master during the past year.

Allowing students to research freely also means that the school community has to be ready to be a subject of that research. When SLA students need data about human behavior or beliefs, they often distribute online surveys via the schoolwide memo or their personal networks. Teachers in particular are a regular source for personal interviews. One Spanish project even had students interviewing school staff about their dream houses for a project that involved practicing domestic vocabulary. Because every class participates in active research like this at one point or another, there is a sense of reciprocity in helping students with their own work. The school is game to answer questions (and students are also coached about when information should be collected anonymously).

SLA's Academic Integrity Policy (see Appendix C) helps create a unified culture of research by setting the same expectations and consequences for plagiarism across the curriculum and grade levels. The baseline of the policy is that a student must redo any plagiarized work in order to continue in the course. Students review this policy on the same day each year, with a longer introduction for freshmen, and they are required to sign an acknowledgment that they understand and will follow the policy. This takes the guesswork out of plagiarism issues for both students and parents.

Back to the Beginning

When students in Matthew VanKouwenberg's classroom are throwing airplanes across the room, they are reviewing the scientific method and lab procedures. By adding and removing design elements from their planes, students discover that changing more than one variable at a time means that they are not building a controlled experiment. Research methods must be exact in order to be effective. However, the biggest goal of the activity is to get students to check their own assumptions as they research. VanKouwenberg explains:

> Students assume that things given by teachers (or any directions or many authority figures, for that matter) are correct/good, but sometimes they are not in huge ways. In order to do good research you need to be aware of your assumptions, often citing them at the beginning so other people can norm their assessments. Since they're often so focused on the fun part of the activity, they gloss over the directions, not realizing the underlying assumptions that affect the way in which they interact within the world.

These assumptions can come out of the rush of excitement. They can also come from deep-seated beliefs and stereotypes. If students are going to engage in authentic research, they must also be able to look inward and explore their own unconscious inclinations and blind spots—and then evaluate the weaknesses in the content of others. VanKouwenberg leads students to this practice with a self-knowledge question posed after the activity is done: *How would you improve this experiment?* In a classroom that values authentic student research, even the methods of the teacher are eligible for scrutiny.

STUDENT PERSPECTIVE: RESEARCH

Sam Lovett-Perkins, Class of 2013

There is a point in every high school millennial's life that is truly frightening: the moment you realize Wikipedia can't help you. The information and the terms used become too complex, and you are forced to turn to other sources—real sources—to get the information you need.

This exact situation happened to me during my senior year, when our science class was commissioned by the Chemical Heritage Foundation to create legislation that would promote the sustainable usage of plastics. I started looking for complex texts about the industry, and Wikipedia seemed like the fastest and simplest way to get the project done. But as I tried to muscle my way through the assignment, I found the reading incredibly difficult. Terms like "thermosetting polymers" and a "semi-crystalline amorphous structure" thwarted my greater understanding of the topic I was researching.

As the time for presentation approached, I realized I'd have to try something else. I started my research again, asking the most simplistic of questions: What is a plastic? Where are they found? How are they being used? These were the inquiries that informed my research. I scoured the Internet, looking for documents and pages that answered these basic questions. Informational websites and videos made for the general public provided the basis of my research, and from there I could move into specifics of the scientific and industrial applications of plastics. I also utilized real live sources, including a teaching assistant from Drexel University and my SLA teacher.

From inventory charts to scientific research papers, I had access to a large quantity of information through the Internet. But the project taught me how to filter that knowledge. Even though I could force my way through a complex scientific abstract about the construction of thermoplastics, if I did I wouldn't really be learning. The mix of professional and general resources I ended up using brought me to a more cohesive and complete understanding, which in turn made it easier to form my conclusions when it was time to construct the presentation.

4 Integrating Collaboration

Schools are not designed for collaboration.

Take a look at any traditional learning environment, and it's impossible to ignore the evidence supporting this conclusion. Desks are set in rows facing the teacher and specifically arranged to prevent students from looking at the work of their peers (because that would be cheating). Course sequences divide the sciences from the humanities, and then drill the subject areas down further into subsections that ignore the integrated nature of knowledge and learning. Tests and quizzes require that students work by themselves, and that work is only for the teacher to look at. Even a strict field trip policy can inhibit collaboration; what's meant to keep the students safe can have the side effect of keeping them in a vacuum.

Contrast this scenario with pretty much any work environment seen as successful or desirable today. Law firms, hospitals, design firms, and research laboratories all expect their employees to have great individual capabilities. However, the employees must use those skills in concert with others while working on common projects, whether it's crafting an argument for a case or a course of treatment for a patient. Few professions operate in isolation, and even if the work is done solo, a collaborative review typically takes place before the work is declared done.

It's important to note that collaboration goes way beyond just being able to work well with others. True collaboration means that all parties involved have a stake in both designing and implementing the project. Good interpersonal skills certainly make collaboration easier, but it is the nature of the work that makes collaboration possible. Unfortunately, students are not typically given the opportunity to engage with their studies on this level. Students learn the norms of social propriety in the early grades—share the crayons, don't hit your neighbor, do what the teacher says—and then those skills are used to keep order in the upper grades, when students are kept busy working at their own desks, with their eyes on their own paper.

Students are not the only people in schools hemmed by this anti-collaboration mindset. Teachers are expected to stay within the confines of their subject specialty, and sometimes their curriculum or even their daily lessons are scripted by an outside source. Each teacher contributes to a student's education, but teachers are typically not given time to interact with their colleagues who are working with that same child. Many schools also have a closed-door mindset, with teachers working in fear of the administration—or, worse yet, refusing to share resources and ideas with their colleagues in order to keep the competition at bay.

All of this is to say that teachers have many hurdles to overcome when seeking to encourage collaboration in their classroom. The good news is that students are, in fact, naturally collaborative and willing to share. What they need is the time and space to have that process happen in a meaningful way. And, new digital tools can make some of the messier parts of working together easier to navigate.

Qualities of Successful Student Collaboration

To be successful, student collaboration must have at least three qualities. It must be *documented*, *asynchronous*, and *classroom-based*. Let's consider each of these in turn.

Documented

One mark of a successful collaboration is that the contributions of each member become a cohesive whole in the final product. In some cases, distinctive touches can be attributed to an individual who worked on the project, but not in a way that detracts from its beauty or functionality. In many cases, the individuals are acknowledged with a byline or a credit at the end—or, in many cases, no recognition at all. Whether the collaborators like it or not, the entire process of collaboration that went into the work disappears once the process is complete.

The fact that individuals can come together and produce something greater than the sum of its parts is beautiful. However, the fact that the process itself is so ephemeral can be vexing to teachers, who often want hard evidence of a student's work. Moreover, students deserve a chance to reflect on this valuable part of their education. How can the planning and conversation between students during an authentic collaboration be captured and assessed?

The answer lies in documentation. In its most basic format, collaboration is an exchange between two people. This exchange is typically verbal and also typically unrecorded, which means the moment of collaboration is lost as soon as it ends. One can hope that a participant gained something from the collaboration and will hold onto that knowledge and apply it later. But a *documented* collaboration means that students are able to refer back to those fleeting moments and make sure nothing is lost in translation.

This requirement does not mean that students should go about recording *all* of their academic interactions for fear that they'll forget some relevant detail. But the benefits of collaboration can be greatly increased if the collaborative effort can be captured at key moments in the process. Whether instituted by the student or the teacher, documentation allows students to maximize the usefulness of the individual moments, as well as reflect on their methods of collaboration as the documentation grows in size.

➤ **The digital connection.** The simplest way to document collaboration is to write it down. Digital recording tools provide a wealth of variations on this theme, making it easy for students to capture and store relevant moments. Whether it's making an audio recording of verbal feedback, typing notes during a planning session, or capturing screenshots of online work, students should be encouraged to "make a copy" of the moments that matter.

A secondary bonus to documenting collaboration online is that it can be shared beyond the immediate project partners. A successful moment of teamwork can be pulled up for the whole class to see. Additionally, a collection of group brainstorms can be analyzed for deeper themes and patterns. Documentation that is accessible can enrich the work of others.

Asynchronous

Call forth a mental picture of great collaboration and your thoughts will likely turn to an image of a group working together in person, creating something worthwhile in that moment. A composer and a lyricist by the piano, crafting a score for a new musical. A jury at a round table, deliberating so that they can reach a verdict. Town residents laying down sandbags to keep out rising floodwaters. Whether in pursuit of beauty, justice, or survival, collaborative moments like these are a key part of the human experience—not to mention important for our survival.

There's one catch, though: not all of this work happens simultaneously. Each of the three scenarios just described also required significant legwork outside of the moments of collaboration. The lyricist and the composer likely prepared ideas for their composition before meeting, and they will continue to work on their respective pieces when they are apart. A jury must absorb the testimony presented in a trial, during which time they are actually barred from interacting with each other. Even a sandbagging operation needs some kind of advance planning and setup (unless participants are trying to design the barrier on the fly, in which case the town is probably in trouble). The image we have of people in the thick of their work together, butting heads at one moment and high-fiving the next, is not inaccurate but is certainly oversimplified. Good collaboration involves work done separately as well as together.

So, for students to collaborate well, they need a good reason to work together, some moments to hash it out in person, but also some time to process the collaboration on their own and contribute at their own pace. Moreover, a good project should inspire students to continue their efforts after the class time has ended. A part of every live collaboration session should be used to determine what kind of work should be done separately.

➤ **The digital connection.** For asynchronous collaboration to be successful, students need a shared venue where they can easily access each other's work. This common touchstone prevents individuals from spinning off into their individual orbits and thereby saves time when the group comes back together. Good documentation, of course, supports this practice. Sharing the documentation gives group members the flexibility to explore ideas on their own without getting lost.

The most important support for asynchronous collaboration is the "anchor" document, which outlines the requirements for the project as well as the expectations and roles of each of the group members. For authentic collaboration, this anchor document is best developed by students themselves, and it can take the form of a proposal, a contract, or an outline (more on creating these documents later in the chapter). After the anchor, students may need a variety of shared spaces to collect relevant materials—a spreadsheet for data, a file-sharing site for media, and so on.

Classroom-based

The previous two qualities of successful collaboration may make it sound like the entire process can be computerized. This is not the case. Although online tools can enrich and expedite the collaboration process, person-to-person interaction should be the bedrock of students working together.

Why? Simply put, you empathize more when you're in the presence of the person you're working with. Authentic collaboration is more than just an assembly line, with each worker producing his part in isolation and then connecting the pieces at the end. Authentic collaboration requires a complex and often sensitive level of engagement. Students have to listen to the ideas of others and give up some of their own plans for the good of the group. They have to work hard for their partners, with the understanding that their partners will work just as hard for them. In class, I sometimes describe this process as "entering a covenant." When students begin a small collaboration, such as a day of peer editing, they literally have to shake hands at the beginning of the process—and also assess each other's effectiveness at the end. This sense of reciprocity can be transferred to online interactions, but it is difficult to engender that kind of feeling without a personal touch. Even professional collaborations that begin online often "upgrade" into real life, whether at a conference or an arranged meeting. Meeting face to face keeps students engaged as well as accountable. The asynchronous moments of collaboration should always lead back to work in the classroom.

You now have a sense of the hurdles a classroom must overcome to implement authentic collaboration, as well as a few key qualities of what can make it successful. The framework outlined in the next sections puts a special focus on what you can do within your classroom to facilitate collaboration.

A Framework for Classroom Collaboration

The following four statements summarize the framework for classroom collaboration:

- Model collaboration on a daily basis.
- Spend time on the set-up.
- Monitor progress, and allow students to police themselves.
- Connect beyond the classroom.

These statements are expanded upon in the sections below.

Model collaboration on a daily basis

The value of this practice cannot be overestimated. If the design of the learning environment emphasizes individual achievement in isolation, then students will never develop the skills needed to work together. Collaboration needs to be integrated into the regular routines of your classroom.

As discussed in the introduction to this chapter, the room layout sends the most basic and immediate message about what students are expected to do. Most classrooms at SLA have their desks set up in small groups, and the lessons are designed to take advantage of that arrangement. In his math classes, Brad Latimer has students working together on the warm-up problem, which one table then presents to the class by writing on the board. English teacher Matt Kay labels these groups "pods" and uses them for a variety of tasks—to discuss the previous night's reading, to prepare for a quiz, or even to play a game. These tasks are alternated with individual and whole-group activities, but when students hear the phrase "get in your pods" they know to return to their assigned groups, which switch each quarter.

These small groupings allow students to practice working toward a common goal in a low-stakes setting. However, creating a collective product is not the only way that students can work together meaningfully. When students truly embrace the spirit of collaboration, they will also work to aid each other's academic progress. In the daily classroom routine, this collaboration often takes the form of students sharing their expertise with their partners, whether it's talking through last night's problem set or troubleshooting a problem on a computer. Normally these tasks would fall exclusively to the teacher, with students often giving up and just sitting there until they get the help they need. In a collaborative environment, the teacher still provides ample support when the entire group hits a wall they can't scale. But students know to turn to their peers before they ask the teacher for assistance. This protocol works because the students legitimately care about helping their peers—plus they have learned that being able to effectively explain what they are learning is proof of mastery.

One particular way that students engage in this reciprocal support is via peer editing and review. When working on an individual essay or project, students are often given a deadline for a rough draft and then are required to trade work with a classmate and go through a review checklist. The primary benefit, and the one most tangible for the student, is guided feedback for the project. However, what students give while participating as reviewers also benefits them. Because the peer editing reviews the expectations for the project, it may clarify any misunderstandings the students have. And it also gives students a chance to observe different variations on the project, which might inform their own work. (Note that this kind of peer review is appropriate only when students are allowed to personalize their work; otherwise, sharing rough drafts could amount to cheating.) This process has higher stakes than daily collaboration, but it can still be engineered as a safe space for students to work together. English and history teacher Joshua Block uses peer editing for a variety of projects, including when students write one-act plays. Before the editing begins, Block reviews a detailed protocol for the editing, including what kind of comments are most helpful and how students should be thorough while still treating the work they are reading with respect. When students are taught to remove judgment when they review, it is then possible for them to "provide deep insights into work," Block says, while still engaging the author.

MAKING THE SHIFT

1. Look back: Take a look at one week's worth of daily lesson plans in your curriculum. Who do the students interact with during the course of a class period? If the majority of interactions are with the teacher, or there are no interactions at all, it's time to retool the activities so that students can do the work in pairs or small groups. Replace tasks done in isolation with ones that allow students to support each other's learning.

2. Diagram: How is your classroom arranged? What kinds of activities does that arrangement support? What kinds of activities does it prohibit? Seating arrangements can always be changed, but the "default" arrangement sends a strong message about whether collaboration is valued in your classroom or not. Figure out a way to reflect your updated lesson plans in the physical layout of your seating.

Spend time on the set-up

Integrating collaborative skills into a class's daily routine is an essential stepping-stone to prepare students for group work that is more involved. However, this does not mean that students should be left to their own devices when handling large-scale collaborations. In some ways, the most important phase of a group project happens before the students even start their work. The more thought that teachers put into classroom structure, the more likely that structure will sustain students and give them the solid framework they need to succeed.

At the most basic level, this approach means giving students clear examples of how to work with each other. When he first introduces the concept of "pods" to his freshmen, English teacher Matthew Kay starts with the basics: talking about last night's homework. As for motivation, Kay reports that students "don't need to have much other incentive besides the opportunity to discuss the reading." Pods are not assigned their own group projects; instead, they support individual work through reading reviews, peer editing, and by serving as teams for games. This prepares students for more involved collaboration later in their high school careers.

When it comes to getting ready for major collaborations, teachers can provide support by describing the specific roles students can play in the project. Math teacher Erin Garvey emphasizes that this process looks different depending on how much previous exposure students have had to collaboration. When she teaches 9th graders geometry, she often breaks down a group project into parts that can be completed by each individual. As students progress up the math sequence, she still requires this division of labor, but eventually the students are tasked with splitting up the work on their own, and they are held accountable for their individual roles when they turn in the finished product.

English teacher Alexa Dunn provides a similar framework for independent reading in both her freshman and senior English classes. Students participate in a "book club" with peers grouped by which title they select. The club is provided with a list of roles, and each group member selects a different job for the weekly meeting—manager, questioner, researcher, and so on. The role of note-taker is particularly important in Dunn's classroom, because those students type and then post the group's findings to an online forum. This provision allows her to easily observe what groups have accomplished and to push thinking ahead either on the forum or during the group's meetings. The notes also allow the conversation to continue online, with time given for students to comment on and push the thinking of groups reading other titles.

Another place where teachers can provide structure is in the schedule. No project can be successfully completed if the only deadline in place is the final one, so teachers must determine how many "mile markers" will guide students without overwhelming them. For freshmen at SLA, this often involves quick, daily check-ins in class; seniors, by contrast, are often asked to propose their own schedule, with perhaps one rough-draft deadline set for the entire class. Dunn's book club splits the difference by giving students a weekly meeting time and a final deadline, but asking them to determine the pace at which they will read. No matter who's setting the boundaries, the collaboration should be structured enough so that all group members have a clear sense of their individual responsibilities during each meeting. This approach makes it possible for both the group and the teacher to monitor progress, which will be discussed in greater detail in the next section.

MAKING THE SHIFT

1. Brainstorm: What collaborative skills do your students already have? You can determine this not only by looking at the curriculum of the school, but also by talking to them about their personal experiences. Sports, jobs, and family roles often endow students with abilities that aren't used in the traditional classroom. Figure out where they are in order to effectively plan where they can go.

MAKING THE SHIFT—*(continued)*

2. Analyze: What kind of work will it take to complete a group project that you've designed? Create a roadmap for how students could get from the opening instructions to the finish line. Then, based on your brainstorm, decide how much of that roadmap you need to provide to students in advance. Do they need a predetermined list of roles, or would one model plan be enough for them to create their own? (If the project has a lot of variables, consider making more than one model to share with students; this reminds them to embrace variety and discourages them from basing their own path too closely on your example.)

Monitor progress, and allow students to police themselves

Once you have assigned the groups and introduced the set-up, it's time for students to actually get from concept to product. This is when collaboration can get messy. Even the most carefully designed project can come crashing down on students if the group gets off track or experiences discord. Suddenly the motivated students are attacking the procrastinators, and productivity has ceased. Teachers are left with a conundrum: Are students permanently bound to their groupmates, no matter how bad the situation gets? At what point does it make sense to intervene?

As with every aspect of modeling collaboration, this process needs a level of scaffolding commensurate with the students' own comfort level with group work. For students new to collaboration, sometimes it helps to keep responsibilities more separate than combined. This approach edges toward the "assembly line" model, but it can serve as a middle ground between isolation and authentic collaboration.

Math teacher Caitlin Thompson uses this approach when her Algebra 1 students complete their first project, producing the blueprint of a house by working in groups of three or four. "Each group has to decide which rooms will be in the space," she says. "Then each student is solely responsible for one room with 5–7 pieces of furniture.

The students individually show that they can convert and scale measurements using their mathematical skills in proportional reasoning. They then collaborate to sketch their rooms together—ideally in one visually pleasing and mathematically correct blueprint."

The project requires students to work together at the beginning and end, with ample time in class to both write the proposal and create the sketch. The bulk of the project, however, allows for individual accountability and a chance for the teacher to assess each student's skills. Most important, Thompson keeps the collaborative aspect of this project low-stakes by not penalizing a group if the house is still "under construction" after the deadline—meaning a group member fell behind on completing the calculations for a room. She can then give the struggling student guidance without holding the rest of the group hostage. This provision keeps anxiety low while students are getting used to the collaborative process.

By the time SLA students are juniors, more emphasis is put on group accountability, but that doesn't mean that students are stuck with each other permanently. Physics teacher Rosalind Echols gives students more opportunities to design their collaborative environment, but that also means that they are the ones who have to intervene if the going gets tough. Each quarter, students submit group member preferences, listing three students they work well with and two they do not. Based on these requests, they are then placed at tables where they will remain for the quarter. When it is time to begin work on a project, students must complete a group contract. The first step of this process requires them to share their contact information as well as self-identified strengths and areas for improvement (both academic and personal). This contract then gives each member a role—liaison, secretary, arbitrator, and monitor—as well as a requirement to brainstorm rules beyond the three mandated for all groups:

- Each team member must fulfill his or her individual duties every day.
- Each team member must complete homework assignments as assigned.
- If a team member is to be absent, he or she must contact teammates *before* the beginning of class *and* make arrangements to

compensate for her or his absence. Absence does not eliminate the team member's responsibilities.

The next section of the contract is labeled "Steps for Firing a Group Member." Echols's one requirement for this part of the process is that the entire group must meet with her, but students can add additional steps as they see fit. They often add an opportunity for a warning or check-in for students who are slacking off. (For the contract template, see Appendix F.)

The opportunity to "fire" a peer amuses many students, and they often throw around the threat during the early phases of a project. However, when conflicts do arise, groups rarely get to the point where they actually vote to kick out a group member, largely because the protocol is actually designed to address and resolve group dysfunction. If anything, the firing process reveals the poor collaborative efforts of the students bringing the complaint. If students wait until the last minute to seek an intervention, they have probably been frustrated with their group member for a long time and want to dump the problem instead of solving it. Echols then sits in for what she calls a peer mediation. With her help, the group revisits their contract and students have time to explain what they are accomplishing, without accusation. She then asks them: What kinds of steps are you going to take so that your group can make progress? This way, the responsibility is placed on all members.

Once that conversation is initiated, Echols finds that groups work out their differences—at least to the point where they can function together and get the work done. The result is that students put real effort into the collaboration itself, as opposed to abandoning collaboration in the name of efficiency. The only instance in which a "firing" has taken place is when a student is chronically absent and not compensating for it. Echols then automatically intervenes and helps that student complete a project alone.

It's crucial to mention that although these tools all help students manage their own collaborative dynamics, the teacher cannot just sit back and relax as students get down to work. As English and history teacher Joshua Block noted in an article published by *Edutopia*, one of the essential guidelines for teachers facilitating group work is to "be aware!" He goes on to explain the many ways that he monitors the dynamics of groups in his classroom:

> I maintain a constant awareness of the dynamics and the physical language of individuals around the room, even when I am far away from a group. I make mental notes about which groups are communicating effectively and which groups are dominated by one or two individuals. I take note of who is sitting separately from other group members. (Block, 2014)

This level of teacher engagement allows teachers to support student collaboration without overtly managing it. Students should be encouraged to resolve conflicts on their own, but the teacher can also massage group dynamics to avoid major fallouts before they happen.

MAKING THE SHIFT

1. Assess: How much ownership do your students currently take of their own learning? Are they ever asked to reflect on their own strengths and weaknesses as a student? Students must be able to complete these individual assessments before they can effectively work with others. Give students language to identify the key aspects of their learning personalities: Big-ideas person? Detail-oriented? Taskmaster? Procrastinator? Have them share these parts of themselves whenever they get into groups.

2. Design: Make sure your project design meets students where they are in terms of accountability. Based on the level of metacognition evidenced by the activity outlined in the preceding step, create a set of expectations for how individuals and groups will be assessed. Assign clear deadlines and point values to each responsibility, and make sure that students know where the "safety valve" is to keep anxiety levels down.

Connect beyond the classroom

One of the best ways to make collaboration meaningful for students—and also to encourage professional conduct from them—is to have them work with groups outside of their school setting. Sometimes this is as simple as connecting with individuals in the "real world," like interviewing a family member or calling a government office. These situations enable students to practice proper etiquette, a necessary skill for working with others. The next level of collaboration, however, asks students to build something with those outside parties, instead of just collecting information from them.

Some outside groups work with students as an explicit part of their mission. English and history teacher Joshua Block, for example, has partnered with Philadelphia Young Playwrights for several years. His students write one-act plays in class and receive instruction from a professional playwright, who both does lessons in class and provides personalized feedback online. Students whose plays are selected for production then go through a more rigorous revision process and eventually see their works staged by drama students from an area university. These plays are never just written in isolation; students are expected to consider the feedback of both their peer editors and the visiting playwright.

Collaboration beyond school can be taken to the next level when students are positioning themselves as the professionals. This approach works especially well for courses that have students learning computer or audiovisual skills, where teens often outpace adults when it comes to mastery. For digital video teacher Doug Herman, teaching students the basics of how to shoot and edit footage is only a piece of the puzzle, which is why he has helped foster the growth of a student-run media production house directly out of the classroom. Rough Cut Productions has been working professionally since 2010, with clients ranging from City Hall to the nonprofit sector, and this provides opportunities for students to fine-tune their professional media skills out in the field, while simultaneously providing a much-needed revenue stream for the continued growth of the program. Students are also extending their reach by teaching online courses in video production for the American School in Bombay, India. Student-produced films and tutorial videos provide both inspiration and guidance for these online students, plus the alumni continue to remain connected and help teach the newest students at SLA. Put simply, these kids own the entire process.

MAKING THE SHIFT

1. Brainstorm: What work do students do that could be supported by experts in this subject, out in the "real world?" Perhaps there are writers who make a living in a particular genre, or mathematicians who regularly use the concepts that students are practicing. At the very least, these professionals can describe their work to students; but perhaps they are willing to participate in real collaboration and give their time and expertise over to helping students improve their own work. Look for ways to connect professionals with student work directly, either by bringing people into the classroom or pushing work out to them online.

2. Brainstorm again: This time, focus on the opposite: What skills are students proficient in that they could take with them out into the "real world?" If the skill is technology-based, there may a demand for their services, especially in the nonprofit and educational sectors (which may appreciate that students are willing to collaborate for free). Another ripe venue for outside collaboration is with younger schoolchildren, because it expands the number of topics that older students can claim to be "experts" in.

Roadblocks and Work-arounds

Student: "My group-mates are not working as hard as me or doing what I tell them to." This is the most common variety of complaint that teachers receive during group projects. Assuming that the student body is not completely homogeneous, there will always be a range of motivation and effort given in any student group. Within that range, a group leader often emerges—and sometimes that group leader becomes frustrated.

A common response to this sentiment is that "good" students should not be penalized for the laziness of their peers, and it does make sense to build controls and safety valves into collaboration, as discussed earlier in this chapter. However, this does not mean that the more capable or hard-working students should be given an automatic out. Few real-world jobs are performed in isolation—and few employees find success by complaining to the boss or asking for a transfer every time one of their coworkers drops the ball. When students are put in a trying group situation, they need to work it out to the best of their ability before an intervention is arranged.

Often this situation is framed in terms of the "slacking" students—what they need to do to step up and meet expectations. This approach deals with only part of the situation, however. A group can be just as hamstrung by a group leader who organizes the project according to her work habits and hasn't considered that this style is not universal. When Echols peer-mediates group work in her physics class, "the students are often complaining that 'they don't work exactly the way I work, and I'm angry with them.' And they've done very little to address the problem."

Both parties need to be nudged toward seeing things from the other side. The students accused of slacking need to have an uninterrupted moment to describe their situation, including when the project went off track, and how *they* would have structured things differently in order to keep the group functioning. The students bringing the complaint then need to seriously consider the proposed alternate plan. Would it suit the group? If not, then where can a compromise be found? Suddenly the leader is taking the needs and feelings of the group seriously.

Student: "We don't have time to meet outside of school." Whether it's distant neighborhoods, complicated commutes, or packed schedules, students face real barriers when trying to get together outside of class time. This situation has a two-part solution.

The first is to be completely transparent with students about how much time the collaboration will take, and also about how much time will be provided in class. Depending on your situation, it may make sense to provide class time for all work that must be done together in person, along with a daily schedule to keep students focused. Make expectations clear at the beginning of the project: "If your group uses class time productively, you'll finish each mile-marker task and won't have to meet on your own." This kind of barometer helps students track their progress even when they are working individually.

The second work-around uses any electronic method of communication that students can get their hands on. Never has "the digital connection" been more useful! As discussed earlier, students should set up an "anchor" document that serves as a landing pad for their proposal, brainstorming, and any individual pieces of work that need to be blended together. This facilitates asynchronous collaboration quite well. In addition, students should choose at least one method of direct communication and establish contact at the very beginning of the project. Echols's group work contract has a place to record contact info and makes several suggestions: phone, Facebook, Twitter, and e-mail. Add videoconferencing to that list, and suddenly students have the same level of connectivity that businesspeople around the world also enjoy. Students don't have to physically be together; they just need to find a moment in time to connect. Facilitate this by requiring them to "set appointments" at the end of an in-class work period, and to record the schedule on their anchor document.

Teacher: "It's impossible to grade this work fairly." This objection reflects a mindset that has not yet opened up to the core value of collaboration. As discussed earlier in this chapter, an authentic collaboration blends student work so that the exact contribution of each group member can no longer be delineated. When this happens, the group has succeeded in creating a project that is greater than the sum of its parts—and their grade and feedback should reflect that success. Likewise, if all the teacher looks for in a student collaboration are the individual contributions, then that is all the teacher is going to get from students.

Modeling Collaboration Schoolwide

Like any skill, collaboration becomes more natural if students practice it beyond the island of a single classroom. The practice of working with others can be expanded in many directions within a school. Here are a few examples from SLA:

- **Across disciplines.** Juniors at SLA participate in a science fiction unit that is supported by their physics and English classes. In physics they must analyze the technical side of a science fiction novel and thoroughly explain the mechanics of whatever spaceship, jetpack, or time machine exists in the text. In English they explore the conventions of short story writing and then write their own story that includes an element of sci-fi.
- **Across grade levels.** SLA has an informal "house" system, with advisories from each grade level clustered together in groups of four, freshmen to seniors. These groups participate in a variety of tasks and events, from ice cream socials to intensive sharing about the college application process.
- **Across course sequences.** Each year, approximately half of the senior class at SLA participates in the school's Student Assistant Teacher (SAT) program. This program places seniors in an underclass course full time, where they provide general support for the teacher. The course is one that the senior has already taken, usually with the same teacher the student is now working with. The student assistants bring a veteran viewpoint to the content, as well as their more advanced skills in that discipline, to a room full of students who are excited to have an expert-peer work with them toward mastery.

To ensure that these cross-school collaborations happen, collaboration must happen between teachers—and this is sometimes the hardest connection to achieve. Between tight class schedules and strict controls on curriculum, it can be difficult to make the time and space for work that goes beyond your individual classroom. The good thing is, it only takes one other willing party to get the ball rolling. Even if it's only two teachers collaborating, students will still be enjoying the benefits of your work together—and that typically gets other teachers on board.

At the very least, you will be modeling authentic collaboration for your students, and this matters as much as any policy you could put in place for group work. Students are tuned in to the atmosphere of their learning environment. Why should they take the time to work with each other if their teachers don't do it themselves? Conversely, when students see teachers who are happily collaborating, the learning environment becomes a place where people want to be.

Back to the Beginning

One of the beautiful things about this framework for teaching and learning is that it was created collaboratively by the very staff that uses it. The founding staff of SLA was hired six months before the school opened its doors and logged many hours working together to design the pedagogical system described in these pages. Because everybody but principal Chris Lehmann was working full-time in another setting, these meetings rarely happened in person. Instead, the staff got together online for 90 minutes once a week. Back in 2005, now-common tools like Google Docs and Google Hangout did not yet exist, so the group used Moodle, the school's original course-management system, and in doing so learned the ins and outs of the system that became the backbone of the school's online presence. Many long hours and one backyard barbeque later, the staff had a general handbook for students highlighting the essential pieces of the culture of the school-to-be. After meeting the incoming class at New Family Night in late spring, the staff then conducted a two-week intensive workshop to hammer out the five core values, a schoolwide rubric, and the gradewide essential questions. Lehmann describes the process as "vigorous, intense, and awesome," with a day and a half spent just on the five categories for the rubric (see Appendix A). District officials who stopped by to check on the group's progress presented a common message: you are doing great things, and you are going to be fine.

According to Lehmann, this process had both an immediate and a long-term benefit. "We did a lot of hard work to make it happen... it reinforced in us what was possible in a collaboration online." After months of blending virtual and in-person collaboration, "it made sense for us to make those online spaces for kids, because we saw how useful it was for our own work process." This spirit of collaboration continues to live on among staff, with a conscious embrace of the long, messy, complicated, but rewarding process. This culture extends to students as soon as they join the community as freshmen.

STUDENT PERSPECTIVE: COLLABORATION

Jesus Jiminez-Lara, Class of 2013

My most memorable moment of collaboration at SLA is not a pretty one. In my 10th grade digital video class, we were assigned to groups to make a short one-minute video representing an emotion. My group would get up and socialize instead of helping me in the video's production. Our teacher had given us three weeks to finish the project, but with our group, we got it done within the hour it was due.

Now, I am by no means a natural born leader. I consider myself a very approachable person, and not bossy at all. But my anxiety about turning in absolutely nothing made me really assertive with my other partners. I found the courage to urge them to collaborate with me, in an authoritative tone. I also convinced them that my grade was not the only one in jeopardy. When the class videos were screened, many people were eager to see their projects. When ours played, our rough project looked like an abstract piece compared to the short narratives everybody else did. It was nothing special, but it did meet the requirements and we got a decent grade.

STUDENT PERSPECTIVE: COLLABORATION—*(continued)*

During my first semester at Temple University, I had an experience with a group project where I was more comfortable being in a leadership position. For my "Media and Culture" class, our final project was to create a product that could take the form of mass media. The group I was assigned to did not talk to each other for the first two weeks, but then I became our liason and made sure we distributed the work evenly amongst ourselves. Our finished product was a magazine for music enthusiasts, which got an "A." The unpredictable nature of collaborative projects in high school helped me communicate better with my peers and keep the project on track. As a result, I am much more capable of handling similar situations. Hopefully, I will resolve future problems way before the hour a project is due.

5 Perfecting Presentation

Not everyone likes public speaking.

This fact comes into painful focus at least a few times a year, whether it's for a middle school student doing a book report in front of the class or a best friend giving the toast at a wedding. People who feel nervous in front of crowds know exactly what can happen: sweaty palms, that deer-in-the-headlights took, and the danger of blanking on what to say next.

These feelings make it sound like some people should be allowed to skip presentation altogether. And yet, the modern workplace demands that every individual be able to speak in front of at least a small crowd. Moreover, even the most stage-shy individuals can succeed at public speaking, as long as they are well prepared and working with content that they know and care about.

Therein likes the rub. The typical modes for presentation in schools rely on superficial content: reciting memorized poems, reading off of a poster, or showing off identical projects. Often these events are trumped up as being big moments for public speaking, staged in the school auditorium with a special audience. But they create a high-pressure scenario without giving students the complete exposure to the many different aspects of good presentation. Students need to go through creating, polishing, and defending a product that reflects authentic learning. It is then that they can best take the stage and speak with confidence.

Characteristics of Successful Classroom Presentations

For this process to be comprehensive, students also need frequent and formative experiences with many different types of presentations. How can this practice be integrated into the classroom so that students learn to show the best version of themselves and their work? The answer is that presentations should be **flexible, shareable, and interactive.**

Flexible

As evidenced by the scenarios just described, "presentation" is too often taken to mean "giving a speech in front of a group of people." In a classroom setting, this translates into students standing at the front of the room and delivering content to their peers. Although this skill is valuable, it's only one variation on the many ways that information can be presented (and, apart from stump speeches and stand-up routines, it's rarely done without any kind of visual aid). Unfortunately, schools sometimes place an exclusive premium on the speaking aspect of presentation, when in fact worthwhile content can be "presented" through a wide range of mediums, whether live or recorded, brief or lengthy, temporary or permanent.

This flexible approach has several benefits. For one, it keeps the class free of the monotony of endless speeches. More important, however, it asks for an extra level of critical analysis from the students. When everybody is asked to work in the same medium, it's easy for students to get bored by the repetition or discouraged when they stuggle in that particular format (while watching their peers excel). When students are given a variety of presentation options, however, they must take on the responsibility of picking what works best for them and their project. This flexibility allows students to present with confidence and also encourages engagement with the work of their classmates.

➤ **The digital connection.** New presentation tools are being debuted on the Internet every day—at such a rate that it's not worth even naming the latest ones in this book. At the very least, students should be encouraged to break out of the PowerPoint cycle and figure out what dynamic online presentation program could bring their content to life. Once students are comfortable with the idea of exploring and assessing the usefulness of different presentation mediums, feel free to also let them choose their own. They will then choose the program that catches their eye or that they feel most comfortable with (and then teach it to you, since you might not be aware of the latest tool they've discovered).

Shareable

Back to the monotony of the in-class presentation—one of the biggest problems is the limited nature of "live" presentation. Moreover, once that presentation is over, the content becomes invisible again, hidden in the mind of the student who did the project and maybe in the notebooks of the class who watched it. Authentic projects can have a live-share component to them, but they should also be designed to stand on their own, after the formal presentation has ended. More specifically, the project should be made available beyond the confines of the class—to other courses, other students in the school, other schools, and beyond. This sharing helps motivate students to fine-tune their presentation skills, because their project is not only going to be viewed by peers who have the same level of content knowledge and background understanding. Suddenly their work needs to convey the message to a more general audience, without them being present to provide an explanation.

SLA Spanish teacher Melanie Manuel embodies this approach with a project that her fourth-year students complete. The project mission is to "Create a mask that reveals who you are and how the many facets of your identity influence how you operate in your life and how you relate to others." After students use recently acquired vocabulary to write a personal essay about themselves, they design papier-mâché masks based on their essays and incorporate printed lines of the text into the design. The final pieces are displayed gallery-style in the hallway outside of the classroom; they are instructive to students studying the language, but also to members of the school community who have little or no understanding of Spanish.

➤ **The digital connection.** Creative iterations of analytical projects are valuable undertakings, but, unfortunately, time and wall space are both limited commodities in schools. Luckily, there are a plethora of digital tools that students can use to easily document and package projects so that the work can live online. More traditional formats, such as essays, can be posted on a class blog or wiki. Live presentations can also be captured with video- and audio-recording tools, allowing students to perfect their delivery on their own time. New tools can also push students toward making projects that are more dynamic, as they decide which medium best conveys the message—perhaps even using more than one, if necessary.

An added bonus to presenting projects online is that it breaks a classroom out of the one-at-a-time model. By setting up a common landing page for finished work, students can "tour" projects online. As in a brick-and-mortar museum, students are not expected to engage with every single piece; instead, they get to give more attention to the work that interests them.

Interactive

The last flaw with traditional presentation is its static format. In many real-world situations, the stakes of a live speech are high because the goal of the speaker is to influence people—to get them to vote, to laugh, to buy. In the typical classroom, however, the only parties who really "care" about the presentation are the presenter and the teacher. Sometimes students have an authentic interest in the content, but more frequently they are preoccupied with the logistics of the assessment, either nervously awaiting their turn or tuned out because they already went. When it's time for questions, an awkward silence ensues, and then eventually the teacher poses questions that help determine a grade.

Teachers may gripe about the lack of engagement during class presentations, but students are not the ones who created this culture. If students are typically creating work that only the teacher sees and never receive feedback from anybody else, why should they suddenly care what their peers think? And why should they give attention to others when that effort on their part is not valued?

For students to care about each other's presentations, they must have a vested interest in the work. Ideally they already have some intrinsic interest in the content, but they can also benefit from a presentation structure in which some kind of interaction is integral to the project's success. This goal can be achieved in a number of ways. One is to allow for interaction *before* the teacher is making the final assessment, so that students can help improve each other's work. SLA math teacher Caitlin Thompson uses this strategy with her Algebra 1 students when they complete a project on systems of inequalities. Students dream up a snack that uses two ingredients and then must create a formula that allows them to determine "the most profitable and desirable combination" for that product. Once all the calculations are complete, Thompson gives each group 20 minutes to produce three slides on their project, and then devotes one class period for students to present *and* reflect on each other's work.

Commenting on her recent experience with this strategy, Thompson says it gave her "a quick chance to review how well students were doing in general on the topic. It was very interesting to see who caught other students' mistakes more quickly and who caught their own mistakes as they were presenting." Students valued the presentations because they were able to give meaningful feedback to each other based on their own proficiency. Thompson was so impressed with their proofreading the first time she did this project that she now schedules presentations to take place *before* students turn in the project for grading—a kind of live rough draft in which the student feedback helps improve the final product.

Another method to encourage interaction is to give students a role in the assessment itself. The simplest way to do this is to have students fill out the grading rubric with comments for their peers as they view the presentations. Teachers can then read and reflect on these comments before giving a grade, agreeing or disagreeing with what the peers said. This approach provides presenters with significantly more commentary than they would receive otherwise, and it also honors students by putting their feedback on the same level as the teacher's.

➤ **The digital connection.** Conveniently, most of the digital mediums that students might use to share their presentations also have built-in tools for interacting with the work. At the very least, students should be encouraged or even required to leave comments for work that has been posted online. If the work is in the draft stage, these could be comments for improvement, or if the work is complete, comments that engage with the arguments and ideas of the project.

Even more effective are projects that incorporate digital tools as an active component of the experience. Instead of just posting a static piece of material, how can students design their presentations so that viewers will actively explore the content? Consider the many ways that companies use online mediums to slowly introduce and engage potential buyers with their products. Students can vary the mediums they use to share material by designing websites that incorporate visitor surveys, audiovisual clips, petitions and pledges, and links to related information. They can share their ideas over time, creating a narrative or even a kind of mystery by pushing bits and pieces out over social media. Social media venues also encourage students' peers to "follow" their projects, both literally and figuratively.

Once students have broken out of the front-of-the-room presentation mold, the possibilities are endless. Of course, this range of options can also be overwhelming for students. The process of creating the presentation should not overwhelm the actual content of the project! The framework described in the following sections includes strategies you can use to personalize student presentations without diluting its purpose.

A Framework for Classroom Presentation

This framework can be broken down into five components:

- Acknowledge two stages of presentation.
- Let students pick the medium.
- Let the presentation influence the outcome.
- Present beyond the school walls.
- Practice on the micro level.

Each of these plays an essential role in the process of making students both comfortable with and proficient in presenting to a wide variety of audiences.

Acknowledge two stages of presentation

As discussed in the previous section, "presentation" is often conflated with public speaking, but to create really fantastic presentations, students need to think about both the product and its delivery.

For this to happen, teachers need to support both aspects of presentation in their classes. First, there need to be explicit expectations for what constitutes a polished product. English teachers at SLA have a poster hanging in their rooms: "Before publishing, make sure that your work is professional and free of errors." In the schoolwide rubric, "presentation" is its own category, and teachers use this section to describe exactly what kinds of errors they will be looking for. When students are in the rough-draft phase, they are often directed back to this rubric, or given an editing sheet that turns the items on the rubric into guiding questions. Peer editing is a cornerstone of practice at the school as well—a collaborative task with the added benefit of letting students hone their own presentations by seeing what their peers have accomplished. Because students are all pursuing their own lines of inquiry, teachers don't have to worry about students "stealing" ideas from each other. (However, stealing presentation tips and tricks from each other is encouraged!)

Once students have gotten edits on their drafts, it is equally important that teachers give them time for revision—and then hold them to a high standard once the work has been submitted. Several SLA teachers will occasionally bestow a "surprise" revision day to students right before a major project is due. Students come in thinking their work is done, but then the teacher does a rapid-fire review of the project, points out additional areas for improvement, and gives them the class period to make changes. By the same token, many teachers have a list of criteria for which they will "bounce back" projects for more editing—for example, a lack of outside sources or basic errors in composition. This high standard is reinforced by the fact that much student work is posted online for public consumption. Teachers are seeking to help students put their best foot forward on the Internet for their general reputation, not just for their grade in the class.

Giving extra attention to the final product ensures that students have work to be proud of. The next step is to make sure that work gets presented to an audience whenever possible. I have mentioned this idea earlier in the chapter, but it bears repeating that in most school environments the only person who sees student work for any length of time is the teacher. Why should students put so much effort into a product that is only going to be viewed by one person? Student work should be put on display—and that often means that the teacher needs to figure out a venue for the presentations to live. That can be as simple as setting up a gallery in the hallway or a landing page for links to projects. At SLA, 11th grade English students have an entire website devoted to their 2Fer essays (the self-directed analytical essays described at the start of Chapter 2). The 2Fer Quarterly (www.2fer-quarterly.org) was founded after students actually requested a way to further revise their papers after teachers gave feedback. At the end of each quarter, students select one of their essays from that marking period, make additional edits, and then post it online. This is a necessary step toward earning their portfolio grade, and it also allows for a "reading day" when students get to respond to not only the writing, but the ideas presented.

For something like an essay, the work usually does not need a separate introduction. Many projects, however, need some kind of write-up or recording for the work to make sense to an outside audience. This step allows students to practice giving context for their work, the same way they would in a verbal presentation, only now that information is preserved for a larger audience to access.

MAKING THE SHIFT

1. Brainstorm: What are your current expectations for a polished, professional project? Without looking at your current project description, do a quick write-up of what flawless student work should look like in your classroom. Then compare it to the

MAKING THE SHIFT—*(continued)*

instructions that are given to students. How do they compare? What are you expecting from students that is not being communicated? Revise and replace language so that your expectations are crystal clear, including what the best work looks like, and the non-negotiable baseline.

2. Make a list: Write down all of the student work that only you, the teacher, see and respond to during the course of the school year. Start by pledging to have students share half of that work with others—whether it's with one other student, the entire class, the school, or beyond. Figure out the appropriate venue for each item, and make sure that you tell students early and often that their creations will be available for public consumption (so they had better make it good)!

Let students pick the medium

A well-designed project sets clear expectations for the content it will cover. Whether it's a set of formulas in math or a social theory in history, students must prove mastery of a particular concept. *How* they present that work, though, can be flexible (although this is not to say that it should be random). Students need to be intentional in the presentation methods they select, thinking about which will be the most effective, as well as where their own strengths lie.

SLA math teacher Sunil Reddy uses this approach with a project for students in his Pre-Calculus course. Groups of students are tasked with researching the evolution of certain relevant formulas. Then they must explain them to the class "in creative ways (not just writing a step-by-step guide that could just be a copied version of what they researched)," Reddy says. The group collaborates on working through the proof, but then each individual student creates his or her own final product presenting the steps of the proof, demonstrating individual comprehension as well as showing off individual flair. Students have created stop-motion animation, puppet shows, and even slideshows narrated by an accompanying rap. Students get to select a medium in which they enjoy working, but they also have to make sure that they have a deeper connection with that format as a learning tool. Reddy explains: "Students have to think hard about which mode of presentation best suits their own learning processes. Subsequently, they can experience how to most effectively teach something back to others using that presentation style."

This approach has the added benefit of allowing students to capitalize on areas of expertise that may otherwise be shut out of their traditional education. The creative arts are all useful here, as are audiovisual skills—and sometimes these skills can be used in concert with each other. Health teacher Pia Martin gets big laughs when she assigns a project asking her students to write and record songs educating the public about different sexually transmitted diseases—but as students get into the process, they also get serious about the content. They research the STD, pick the musical genre, pen the lyrics, rustle up some instrumentation or a backing track, and record a video. The results are catchy, unexpected, and incredibly effective in getting students to talk openly about sexual health.

MAKING THE SHIFT

1. Look back: Review all of your assignment descriptions from the past school year. Did you give students any freedom of choice for their presentation medium? If your answer is no, identify which projects could benefit from having some pre-selected options to choose from. If your answer is yes, identify which project presentations could become 100 percent student-selected.

2. Survey: Poll your students: "What kinds of presentations help you learn the most?" This question can be broken down into questions about different types of knowledge: "What helps you

---

MAKING THE SHIFT—*(continued)*

memorize content?" "What helps you understand complicated concepts?" "What helps you master a new skill?" You may want to clarify that this question is different from "What mediums do you *enjoy* the most?" Ask students not only to name what works for them, but to explain why. Their answers become your list of suggestions for the next project.

Let the presentation influence the outcome

As discussed earlier, too often students deliver their presentations in an apathetic environment, where nobody but the teacher cares about how things are going. Sometimes teachers themselves don't even "count" the presentation as part of the overall grade for the project, making the front-of-the-room speech a meaningless hoop that students must jump through.

At the very least, students should be held responsible for the *quality* of their presentation and not just whether the content contained in that presentation is correct. SLA takes care of this by including "presentation" as one of the five categories in its schoolwide rubric (see Appendix A). However, this only takes care of student engagement on an extrinsic level. Students who care about their grades will be motivated, but what about those who aren't? And what about everybody else in the class who is not being graded at that moment?

One informal way to address this concern was discussed earlier in the chapter: have students present their rough drafts to each other, and turn the presentations into a peer-editing session. If students need to practice their formal presentation skills, however, that presentation should matter for reasons beyond securing a passing grade. On the simplest level, you can turn presentations into a kind of game show, where the audience can vote on which presentation they thought was most effective, or give "best of" awards in different categories once all presentations are finished. This approach elevates students to the level of assessor, a job they often take seriously, even if the awards have no numerical influence on the grades (although they certainly can, if you set that expectation).

This method can go a long way in increasing student engagement, but it also assumes that students are interested in accolades for their own sake (not all students like to be in a pageant). To take student presentation to the next level, the work has to go from token awards to outcomes that matter. Consider that most presentations are seeking to convince an individual or a group to take a certain action. Job candidates enter interviews knowing that they must convince their potential employer that they're more qualified for the job than anyone else. Architects need to convince their clients that their design is the best, just as contractors must convince companies that their bid is superior in both quality and price. Using this model, what are the different ways that students can convince each other to take their side?

A classic method is the simulation. Often organized as a trial or a debate, these presentations ask students to take on a particular role and present their position, sometimes by working towards a common goal, and other times in an attempt to defeat the opposition. Several teachers at SLA use this method, including history teacher Matt Baird, who invites students to hash out the Homestead strike of 1892 by having teams of students represent Andrew Carnegie, Henry Clay Frick, the striking steel workers, the people of Homestead, and the Pinkerton hired officers. The "trial" is a roundtable-style discussion, in which "each group tries to lessen the extent it is responsible for a situation," Baird explains. "Since only 100 percent of the blame can be assigned, you can have multiple groups argue instead of just a simple trial with a plaintiff and defendant." Students activate the knowledge that they acquired during the unit leading up to this activity, but the real fire of the activity comes from engaging with the deeper questions embedded in the conflict: What are the rights of workers? What responsibility does industry have to labor versus profits? With multiple groups defending themselves, the debates can become complex while remaining animated.

Another way to raise the stakes is to give students a chance to influence their future in the class. In my own junior English class, students participate in a project in which they must identify a problem relevant to life in Philadelphia, research the history and causes of that problem, and then convince the class in five minutes that their topic is one of the most pressing issues in our city today. The reason for their pitch? Students will vote on which topics are most important to them, and those will become the choices for our *next* project, in which students will have to identify and design a public information campaign to promote a solution to the problem. During the first round of presentations, students have a ballot that asks them to take a few relevant notes: What's one fact you learned from this presentation that you didn't already know? Why does this problem affect Philadelphia right now? As a result, I rarely have to step in with questions of my own—the student body becomes the board, weighing one issue against another and probing a group that didn't give them sufficient information.

The next level of making a presentation matter, of course, is to take it beyond the classroom—more on that in the next section.

MAKING THE SHIFT

1. Imagine: Take a look at a current presentation that students complete in your class. Engage in this little thought experiment: What if getting a grade was no longer a reason for that presentation? Would students still be motivated to participate? Why or why not? How about the audience? If you can't think of any good answers, this presentation is ripe for an overhaul.

2. Create the motivation: Continue with the assumption that students aren't presenting for a grade. What intrinsic reason will students have for engaging? If possible, allow the presentations to have the purpose of convincing the audience to agree with a viewpoint or take a certain action. Or create a structure in which the students themselves are assessing the work of their peers— either giving accolades to the best final products or giving feedback to rough drafts before they are submitted for a grade.

Present beyond school walls

You have probably already witnessed how dedicated students are when they present in front of a general audience, whether it's through school government, the performing arts, or some other venue. There are many different ways that you can arrange for this kind of presentation for your own classroom—and conveniently, there are also several ways that it can happen without students having to leave the actual school building.

Online presentation. It's easy to have students post their work on a class blog or wiki. What makes this process meaningful, however, is when students have been creating their project with a particular audience in mind and then they target that audience once the content has been posted. Sometimes this process involves a little boost from teachers, who promote their students' work among their own professional learning communities. English teacher Meenoo Rami, for example, tweets out links to projects like the class magazines created by her juniors, providing both a public platform for the students and a curriculum model for other teachers.

Other times, however, publicizing the project is the explicit responsibility of the students. In the Public Information Campaign project that my juniors complete, groups must identify a target audience, set explicit goals for what they will achieve with their campaign, and identify which quantitative data they can use to measure their campaign's success. This means that groups are not only posting their work, but also promoting that work through social media and old-fashioned word-of-mouth—in effect becoming their own publicity managers. (It also means they are motivated to create quality content—otherwise the project won't meet its goals!)

Contests and competitions. Student competitions are often seen as the territory of after-school activities: the sports teams, debate league, and academic bowls. However, students can enter many competitions without belonging to a particular club or team, and participation can be the culmination of a project for all students, instead of a privilege awarded to an invited few.

For this approach to work, teachers have to explore the possibilities available to students in their area, and then also explicitly set participation in the contest or competition as an end goal of the project. Many disciplines at SLA have made this process a part of their annual curriculum. For science, it's applying to local and regional science fairs (in addition to participating in the one at our school); for English, it's writing one-act plays or monologues for competitions sponsored by Philadelphia Young Playwrights, as well as national contests sponsored by groups such as Teen Ink (www.teenink.com) and the Scholastic Art and Writing Awards (www.artandwriting.org); for history, it's sending students to compete in our local National History Day (www.nhd.org), which asks students to develop multimedia projects around a different theme each year. Although not every student in the class ends up getting involved with every competition, the external motivator helps students think about more than just getting the work done; and when some students win, as they invariably will, the entire class can celebrate their triumph.

Real-world professionals. The most direct version of presenting beyond school walls can also be the most meaningful for students. Networked teachers are already accustomed to bringing in experts from the field to talk about the practical applications of a particular course of study, or what it's like to have their job. Flipping the script on this routine can surprise both parties in the best possible way. Instead of sitting back and passively learning from the expert lecturer, what if students have to prove themselves in front of the person who knows a lot more than they do? SLA's science teachers frequently use their professional network for this purpose, from bringing in visiting scientists to connect with students during the freshman and sophomore science fairs to having student designers of bio-walls present their designs to local engineers and horticulturalists.

It's important to note that these presentations often happen either before the project has been turned in or after a grade has been assigned. Outside experts are much less intimidating—and also more useful—when they are tapped for critique and feedback on a project. This is especially true for SLA students applying to college, who are sometimes naïve about how critically their writing will be read by admissions officers. English teachers have assembled a team of outside readers to help students with this transition. Once students have a draft of a particular piece of writing, they are paired with an editor who might be a technical writer, a college professor, a magazine editor, or a published poet. Students are coached on how to approach their reader and then they typically go through several rounds of editing, either via e-mail or in person. Even though the outside readers are not passing final judgment on this work, the process provides a healthy preview of the kind of exacting lens that students can expect colleges to give to their work. When an outside editor tells students that they should scrap their draft and start over, they listen!

MAKING THE SHIFT

1. Brainstorm: What can students create that will matter to an audience beyond their own classroom—and who will that audience be? At the start of each project, identify an audience outside of the school that will be interested in the work, and have students design their project around reaching that group. Better yet, have students decide for themselves who their target audience will be, and then have them justify their methods for reaching that audience when the project is complete.

2. Network and canvas: What individuals and organizations can your students connect with? Talk to your spouse, parents, aunts and uncles, old college roommates, former colleagues, and neighborhood acquaintances. Then, ask all of the teachers in your building to do the same. If you still can't find the professionals you need, approach them cold. The worst thing that can happen is that they say no (and they usually say yes).

Practice on the micro level

Now that you have an idea of the amazing heights to which your students can ascend by presenting beautiful, polished projects to authentic audiences via the mediums that suit them personally, how are you going to get them there? The answer is, one minute at a time. If you backward-map the trajectory of any confident presenter, it begins with that person sharing with very small audiences. SLA teachers integrate this kind of practice into their daily classroom activity—emphasis on "daily." Here are just a few strategies that they use:

- **Think, Pair, Share:** Present a question or problem to students on an individual level, and then ask them to share their response or solution with one other person in the class (usually the student sitting next to them). You can extend this activity by having the pairs share with another pair, or asking a student to report out his partner's comments to the entire class.

- **Speed Learning:** The educational version of speed dating! Students sit in two long rows, with pairs of students facing each other. Students are then given a limited time to interact, usually with one side of the room speaking first (not more than a few minutes) and then the other side providing feedback or commentary. One row then moves over a seat, and the process begins again with a new pairing. This activity is an effective way to give students a snapshot of what the class is thinking. It can serve as a social icebreaker, a way for students to get a feel for project topics, or a rapid-fire way to get some feedback and perspective on their own ideas. It can even serve as a surveying method, with each student asking a different research question and collecting data as the activity proceeds.

- **Scheduled Mini-Presentations:** It's the classic student nightmare: being called up to the board to solve a problem or answer some other (obviously impossible) question, all with the teacher's disapproving glare over your shoulder. How to avoid this horror? Transition the at-the-board experience from a pop quiz to an opportunity for students to teach each other. Students can walk the class through one problem from last night's set, talking through the steps as they go. The same can be done with any reading assignment—pick a relevant quote and justify why it is central to the text, or how it builds upon the previous day's discussion. To take the edge off, create a schedule in advance.

- **Present What You Love:** During independent reading units, English students at SLA complete quick "book talks" or "book sells," encouraging their classmates to pick up the title they just finished reading. Senior science students have "10 percent time," during which they get to explore a topic of their choice and create an informational project that they display, science-fair style, at the end of the unit. Students have to explain *why* they liked the work, but the initial impulse for their presentation is grounded in the fact that they liked it.

MAKING THE SHIFT

1. Calculate: Look at a week's worth of lesson plans for one of your classes. Add up the total minutes that students spend presenting to others. This could include all-class discussion, but ideally, it involves a format in which one or more students are presenting ideas or content that they have prepared with the knowledge that they will be asked to share it with someone else. Is there a venue for presentation in your class every day? And does the total average time equal, say, more than 10 percent of the total time (excluding those big end-of-unit presentations)?

2. Start small: For the first wave of transition, integrate a one-to-one presentation method into each day of the week. For the second week, switch half of those methods to presentations that ask students to present to groups of two or four. A week or two after that, switch one of those days to a scheduled mini-presentation. Now you've got micro practice on a daily schedule.

Roadblocks and Work-arounds

Teacher: "Presenting takes up too much time." Remember that cycling through a slew of individual presentations rarely benefits anybody. For math teacher Caitlin Thompson, abandoning this model has benefits for both teacher and students: "I have found that it is a mistake to always feel like students must 'present' to the whole group in order for 'presentation' to be a part of a project. This can often 'waste' 2–3 class periods at the end of each project. It is better for students to 'share out' in small groups at different points or to conceptualize 'presentation' as different ways of communicating information. This way, students gain skills related to communicating their ideas in formal and informal ways." Presentation should never bring your curriculum to a standstill. It should induce further learning.

Teacher: "Students get so carried away with crafting their presentation that they shortchange the content." This roadblock is the potential downside of letting students choose the medium they want to use for their presentation. You might be providing inspiration to a budding director, composer, or graphic designer, but all of these pursuits require significant technical skill and hours of hard work. How do you prevent the medium from running away with the project?

There are several ways to compartmentalize an assignment so that the technical aspects of a presentation don't overwhelm students. Science teacher Gamal Sherif uses one variation on this strategy during an ethnography project in which students create interactive wikispaces exploring the history and influences of African music on American society. "Early on, one mistake was making this a one-off assignment," he says. "The projects were not as rich because students were busy learning the technology rather than the history." Instead of abandoning the technical side of the assignment, Sherif turned the project into a yearlong exploration, in which students made multiple posts throughout the year. Front-loading the technical skills meant that students could focus on the content as the school year progressed.

Another way to help avoid this roadblock is to have students draft, edit, and revise their content *before* transferring the work to its final medium. English and History teacher Joshua Block has students write "language autobiographies" detailing their personal experiences with language and identity, and only when their paper gets his approval can they move on to turning the ideas of that essay into a two-minute "digital story" complete with photo, video, and voiceover. The same holds true for audio recordings, slideshows, films, and designs; the content should be proofed in a format that makes it easy for editors to make comments and corrections.

Student: "My project isn't as good as theirs." With all of this public sharing of work, comparison on the part of students is unavoidable. Giving students flexibility in presentation mediums can help students avoid this impulse, but invariably some students are going to produce work that is absolutely spectacular, and everybody else's work will shine a little bit less in comparison. If students are sensitive about their abilities, then even a perceived difference in quality can destroy their self-confidence.

The traditional solution to this roadblock would be to pull the curtain down over student work, returning it to the private realm of teachers only. Hopefully this chapter has convinced you that does more harm than good! The better solution does not give immediate results but has a lasting positive impact on classroom culture. Instead of seeing project presentations as a measuring stick for intellect, students need to see it as an expression of explicit skills that they themselves can master with the help of their peers. Students already know who in the class can best explain a math concept, show you how to draw a human figure, or catch your grammatical mistakes on a rough draft. The teacher should acknowledge these "experts" as well—but to identify them as a resource, not to pump up their egos. Those students should be sharing their skills with everybody—not to do the work for them, but to show them how they, too, can become expert. That way, students know they have access to the skills that they may have felt previously were out of their reach. If their final project doesn't stand up to the work of their peers, then it's a reflection of a particular skill set, not their general intellect. And it wasn't because the resources for improvement weren't available to them. As math teacher Caitlin Thompson described, having early "share-outs" of work also lets kids know early in the process how their work compares to that of their peers, and then leaves them with time to make up the difference.

Modeling Presentation Schoolwide

When multiple classrooms adopt the framework described in this chapter, the transition to authentic, intrinsically motivated presentations will be easier for students. Adopting the micro-level activities, especially, will pay off in the long run.

At SLA, a few more programs that encourage presentation skills are built into the four-year sequence. Several are embedded into the freshman elective schedule. Drama class focuses on theater arts, but also the more general practice of public speaking and being comfortable in front of an audience. Art class reviews the skills of drawing, painting, and printmaking, but also discusses the graphic arts, perspective, and what makes good composition. Likewise, technology class talks about Internet privacy and acceptable-use policies, but also provides a crash course in whatever content-creation programs teachers are using (art and technology teacher Marcie Hull polls the staff each year to see if there's anything new she needs to add to the list). Because students are required to take these beginner electives, a base level of skill is ensured for the entire student body by the end of freshman year.

On the other end of their four years, seniors spend the entire year gearing up for the culminating presentation of their high school experience: the capstone project. Due at the same time as finals, the capstone is a self-designed, interdisciplinary project that students complete on their own schedule during the entirety of their senior year. Once the materials have been submitted, every senior must complete a 20-minute presentation in order to pass the course (and, by extension, graduate from SLA). These presentations are a challenge, but also a celebration of all that the student has achieved, and they take place over three days near the end of the school year. The more pride a student has in the project, the bigger the audience: project mentors, advisors, other teachers, fellow seniors, and even underclassmen who have been given permission to leave class and attend.

With all of this emphasis on cultivating student skills, it's important to remember that the presenter is only half of the equation. The entire school community also needs to become a willing audience for the work of its students. Sure, people still need to turn out for performances and tournaments; but connecting with student work also needs to be built into their regular routines. For students, that might mean leveraging community time (homeroom, advisory, or whatever your school calls it) to hear and see presentations from different students. For parents, that means including links to student work in the e-mail newsletter, showcasing it on the school's webpage, or making sure it is visible on back-to-school night. For teachers, it means publicizing student work across disciplines and grade levels at your school, arranging for your students to tour other classes with their work, or have groups visit on presentation days. This is especially effective when, just as with capstone presentations, it's framed as a modeling activity for younger students.

Back to the Beginning

This framework does not promise to make all students love public speaking, but it can give them the tools to handle presentations well, no matter how nervous they might be going in. When students are honestly proud of their work, they will be able to share it with confidence and even joy. It is the teacher's responsibility to support them in their preparation, and to also build authentic venues with relevant outcomes when the presentation is ready to go.

STUDENT PERSPECTIVE: PRESENTATION

Shareesa Bollers, Class of 2010

When I entered SLA as a freshman, I considered myself a great performer and a good writer. However, early on in the grade, I realized that I was struggling to express myself as clearly on paper as I do orally. When I am standing in front of a crowd, I have my facial expressions, posture, vocal inflections, and props to help me perform and present myself eloquently. However, the only prop I had to my advantage in a paper was the 12-point Times New Roman font. Thus, I used similes, elaborate metaphors, and complex syntaxes in my papers to help me "perform" my writing. I developed a habit of writing complex sentences, which sounded beautiful in my head but had little actual meaning. As a result, my papers were returned to me with many "awk," "word choice," or "?" all over them. These corrections drove me to seek out my teacher's help after school to edit and discuss my papers.

Going over my paper, the first question my teacher asked during our conference was, "What do you mean when you say this?" I would answer, and then he would enthusiastically reply, "Write exactly what you just said!" Through these conferences, I began to learn the skill of combining my eloquence with clarity. Being held accountable to presenting myself well on all fronts—written, orally, and visually—taught me how to make my written work an extension of my oral presentations.

I went on to become a literature major in college, where I continued to work on unifying my spoken and written voices. Through constant practice and extensive reading, I realized that the beauty of writing is found in its clarity. My teacher's voice saying "write exactly what you just said" turned into my editing voice that I played on a loop in my head when I faced my greatest writing challenge to date: my 92-page senior thesis, which was supported by an hour-long oral presentation. My education at SLA meant that I was capable of writing such a large body of work. However, it was not until I received an *A* for both my oral and written presentations that I felt that I had indeed found my voice as a writer. After years of practice and struggle, I had finally proven to myself that I could be equally articulate in my oral and written presentations.

6 | Making Reflection Relevant

"If you were to do this project again, what would you change or do differently?"

This question is posed to every student who interviews for a spot at SLA. The school doesn't give an admissions exam; instead, students make a weekend appointment to meet us in person and bring along a project that they are proud of completing. After they talk through their process of doing the project—science fair experiments, short stories, models, and drawings—we ask them to consider the possibility of a different path. Some students have an immediate answer; but most of them need a few moments to think it over, at which point we say, "Take your time! It's not an easy question."

We've known them for 10 minutes, at most, and we're already asking them to engage with the core value of reflection. Quickly or slowly, they begin to mention points that they would like to improve—the fine-tuning that would have pushed the product closer to perfection; spacing out their work schedule because they stayed up all night to meet the deadline; the insightful feedback they got from their teacher, scribbled in the margins in colored ink. In almost every case, the project has already received a grade, so the question is theoretical, which takes the pressure off. The fact that most students need some time to respond, however, reveals that reflection takes time, and also that it is a skill not actively practiced in most learning environments.

With an emphasis on due dates, percentage scores, and the standardized measure of "proficiency," students are coached to hit the mark as best they can and then move on to the next task. Some individual teachers may make an effort to incorporate pedagogical tools that encourage reflection—portfolios of work, for example, or allowing test corrections; but these practices are rarely carried through an entire course sequence or department. When asked, teachers might point out that their punishing workload also deprives them of time to reflect. Many of them know that substantial changes or additions to their classroom practice are either happening during the summer or not at all.

And yet, we all know that meaningful reflection is the only way that we grow as humans—personally, academically, professionally. The popular theories of psychologist Carol Dweck support this: individuals with a fixed mindset, who believe that intelligence is innate, are not nearly as resilient than those with a growth mindset, who believe that the brain can be trained like any other part of the body (Dweck, 2007). Reflection is a vital piece of that mindset—if we aren't given the time or opportunity to identify our own mistakes and why they happen, there is no hope for improvement. This is even truer in an inquiry-based classroom, where the learning is messy and the teacher doesn't always have a vision of each step of the process. It's up to students to reflect on their whole path of learning, not just why they got something right or wrong at the end.

Characteristics of Meaningful Reflection

For student reflection to be meaningful, it must be *metacognitive, applicable,* and *shared* with others. Let's look at each of these characteristics in turn.

Metacognitive

Although it's something of a buzz word, "metacognition" is a state of mind that can be useful for all the core values presented in this book. If students are metacognitive about inquiry, then they're thinking about exactly how they are going to phrase that question; if they're metacognitive about collaboration, then they're considering how their introvert or extrovert personality will affect the group. Metacognition is essentially reflection on the micro level, an awareness of our own thought processes as we complete them. So what does metacognitive reflection look like?

When children are first learning to reflect on their work, their educators use simple prompts to get them thinking: *Do you like what you made? Did you do a good job?* Eventually, they are also asked to consider the process: *What did you learn from this task*? Usually these questions are posed by an outsider—a parent or a preschool teacher, for example—who asks the learner for a simple assessment of the outcome. Metacognitive reflection, however, takes this process to the next level because it is concerned not with assessment, but with self-improvement: *Could this be better? How? What steps should you take?* As a result, metacognitive reflection can be used to develop resilience in the face of a challenge. Many young children (and some adults) will throw down their work when they become frustrated with it, unable to transcend the struggle. By contrast, a student who has learned the value of metacognitive reflection will recognize frustration as a signal to pause and think through the situation instead of plowing ahead with the same approach or giving up entirely.

Of course, there's a danger of this metacognition turning into a kind of feedback loop: *Am I reflecting adequately on my reflection?* The better question to keep in mind is, *How is this reflection going to help me in the future?* In many cases, "the future" is just a few minutes away, but this mindset can also apply to cumulative reflection over a unit, a school year, or a lifetime.

➤ **The digital connection.** Students who are not naturally inclined to stop and think need explicit practices to nudge themselves toward quality reflection—and digital tools to make it easier. Keeping a log of tasks and habits, for example, gives students a rich source of data to mine when reflecting on their progress, and there are many apps that will collect and aggregate this information in accessible and attractive ways. The myriad of daily journals, goal-setting programs, and "productivity" apps help to create a regular time and place for reflection, which students can use toward academic or personal projects. Even using a simple timer can help students chunk out their work so they take a reflective break, and some programs have breaks built into the timer cycle, so that a pause from the work is guaranteed.

Applicable

The reflective question in the SLA admissions interview is a great tool for getting to know the student, but it doesn't do much to actually serve their learning process. It's completely divorced from the setting where the student actually did the work, and besides, the student already completed the project.

This kind of isolated, after-the-fact reflection dominates our understanding of the process. When asked to imagine a person reflecting, you probably conjure up an image of an individual alone, in a comfortable place, staring off into the distance, plaintively contemplating some earlier life event. This scene is likely set at the end of a calendar year, or at the end of a lifetime—or, if you imagined a professional setting, at a retirement party. These kinds of personal reflections contribute to the richness of life, because through them we are able to appreciate how our path has shaped our existence. But what about the life that is still to be lived and the work that is still to be done? Unfortunately, this sentimental notion of reflection for reflection's sake keeps the practice from being used for active improvement in the here and now. Academic reflections, for example, often take place at the very end of the course, when both the professor and the student will be moving on to other courses and teaching loads. Students are not typically asked to consider how their performance evolves over the years either. Even though teachers often have a very clear notion of how the curriculum builds on itself and how students must develop their skills in a particular sequence, they often keep this structure hidden from their students. Occupied with the daily grind of delivering curriculum, it often doesn't occur to them that their students might benefit from seeing the big picture.

If this structure is revealed to students, though, then they suddenly have a framework for assessing how their past performance will influence their future work. By being transparent about future tasks and assignments, teachers remind students that they're going to have to use at least some of these skills again, so there's no sense in making the same mistakes. Reflection suddenly has a real and immediate purpose: You know where this course is going, so how are you going to improve the quality of your own journey?

➤ **The digital connection.** If students are going to really benefit from their reflections and apply them to future work, those thoughts have to get out of their heads and into some form of documentation. Proximity here is key; reviewing a previous reflection can be most instructive when students are working on the next task, so their reflection should be stored wherever that work is happening. Paper portfolios can approximate this, although that method forces students to carry a year's worth of work and reflection with them at all times (which is why most teachers choose to keep portfolios in the classroom—logical, but limiting). By contrast, online homes for student reflection are universally accessible and can be organized to accompany student work, so that the past reflection is right in front of students as they start a new task. Digital tools also provide different mediums for students to capture their thoughts—they can type or tag, or talk into the microphone or camera.

Electronic tools of analysis can also play a big role here. Just as athletes track their physical performance using a specific set of metrics, students may benefit from reviewing their academic achievements in different areas, like the categories of a rubric or a list of discrete skills. When used by outside forces as the exclusive criteria for judging a school, this kind of "data-driven" approach can be myopic, but when used by students as one of several tools for measuring success, the process can be empowering. The standards-based grading movement has a multitude of resources available online, including free online grade books for teachers. By tying a numerical score to specific skills, students are naturally encouraged to reflect on their past performance so that they can improve the work, not just the grade.

Shared

Let's go back to that image of the lone person lost in reflection. Once they are done collecting their thoughts, who are they going to share them with? Most likely a trusted confidant or private journal—a safe place with no chance of betrayal. This tendency toward secrecy is natural. In the interest of keeping up appearances, we don't really like to share our weaknesses and past failures (although we do love gawking at the problems and misfortunes of others). But if we are really seeking to take action based on our reflections, then we will likely need some help, and that means we have to own up about what needs work. To make students comfortable with this practice, the classroom has to become a place where each student is recognized as being on an individual path of improvement—and, an important point, no student has reached the end of the path, because *there is no end.* And if there is no finish line, it becomes more difficult for students to compare their relative positions on the journey.

Once that culture has been established, the classroom can become a place of collective support instead of individual competition. By sharing their reflections on their academic work, students can both advise and seek help from their peers. Sharing their achievements helps those who struggled with that particular task, and sharing their weak spots helps them troubleshoot as they work through a problem set or have a peer edit a rough draft.

➤ **The digital connection.** Just as electronic tools make reflections easy to access for an individual, so, too, do they make it easy to share. Sharing becomes instantaneous when material is available online; the collection of commentary from an entire class can also be indexed, searched, and organized by theme—a feature that may be of great use for the teacher, who will want to look at both individual goals and the class's experience as a whole. If students are sensitive about sharing their reflections, the work can also be posted anonymously. Like writing in to an advice column with a pseudonym, the practice allows them to receive guidance and support without embarrassing themselves.

A Framework for Student Reflection

When planning for student reflection, the following four guidelines can help to ensure successful outcomes:

- Put reflection first.
- De-emphasize grades.
- Integrate student and teacher reflection.
- Let reflection accumulate.

Put reflection first

This statement may seem counterintuitive, especially because reflection is the *last* of the five core values presented in this book. And yet, the best way to prevent reflection from being a useless after-thought is to literally put it at the beginning of the learning cycle.

Putting reflection first can be facilitated by the practice of goal setting. Every teacher at SLA has a personal variation on this cycle, but everybody returns to the central idea that the practice of setting goals provides a clear metric whereby students can reflect on their progress. The proposals and contracts described in Chapter 4 are their own kind of goal setting, as both the students (and eventually the teacher) will refer to them once the project is complete. Once this big goal is set, students can also benefit from setting goals for each step of the process. The text that follows describes three different pieces of that process, each from a different member of the SLA science department.

Stephanie Dunda has students set individual goals during every work period for a collaborative project. At the end of each session, the group must confer and divvy up a set number of points between the group members, typically giving out equal points if everybody met goals of similar weight, and shifting the distribution depending on the degree to which a group member exceeded or fell short of a goal. This immediate reflection gives students a useful vehicle for communicating with each other, but it also gives them "quantitative data of what they actually contributed to the project," says Dunda. That data is useful for both teacher and student once the final product is submitted.

This kind of integrated goal setting has the added bonus of allow-ing students to personalize their work schedules. As science teacher Matthew VanKouwenberg points out, "Because they're doing individ-ual projects, different groups are at different places after the initial steps of creating their learning plan." Even when projects have iden-tical steps, students work at different paces; when the projects are self-designed, the idea of keeping students on some sort of standard-ized schedule is even less realistic. But how can a teacher manage the sometimes chaotic reality of 30 different timelines? VanKouwenberg employs online forms that students must fill out at the start and the end of class: first to set the goals for what they will accomplish that hour, and then to rate themselves and talk about what got them off track (or helped them focus).

Of course, even when reflection happens at the end of a unit, it can still be hooked around for students to benefit from later. Science teacher Tim Best arranges the sequence of this process so that his stu-dents get the most out of reflections. His advice is to "ask a few guided questions about a recently completed project. Include things like 'What advice would you give students for next year?' Then have them go back and read that reflection later, as they're starting a new project."

MAKING THE SHIFT

1. Brainstorm: What skills or practices would you like students to be able to self-monitor and improve on their own, or at least actively seek help with? List as many as you can, and then see if they can be organized and prioritized to any degree. These are the skills that you will need to explicitly mention when it's time to have students set goals and reflect on their progress.

2. Observe: When students reflect on their work, what kind of language do they use? Take a look at a class set of current writ-ten reflections, or engage the class in a discussion about their work (and record it). Do they talk about their work with a fixed

---

MAKING THE SHIFT—*(continued)*

---

mindset or with the belief that they can grow? The more they talk about "strengths" and "weaknesses," the more work you will need to do in changing their views about their own abilities. Start by turning "weaknesses" into "areas for improvement."

De-emphasize grades

Earlier in this chapter, I discussed the human tendency against sharing our perceived weaknesses. Students are not exempt from this behavior, and their reluctance is reinforced by the simplistic nature of numerical grades. When teachers hand back a major assignment, one question begins to fly around the room: "What'd you get?" The students who earned a high score confidently show off their papers, and the ones who didn't quietly shove the work into their backpacks (or, sometimes, make a scene of crumpling it up into a ball and throwing it in the trash). When the only thing that students see is a number, it's hard for them to get past how well they measure up. As mentioned earlier, this mentality is reinforced by practices such as standardized testing and class rank. With these sytems in place, how can a teacher get students past this yardstick mentality and focused on their own learning growth instead?

The answer lies in the presentation. Although grades are probably a necessity in your learning environment, there are several ways to produce that data without showcasing it.

Withhold it. Let students see the qualitative feedback first—comments from teachers and students. Require them to complete their reflection on the work before they are allowed to see the numerical grade. This approach has the bonus of asking students to evaluate the work on its own terms, instead of tacked to numerical values.

Leave it in pieces. When filling out a rubric, give students feedback and a numerical grade for each category, but don't bother adding up the total for them. If students really want to know, they can add it up themselves (or wait to see the numerical total on their grade report). This tactic encourages students to begin thinking about their performance on individual categories, and this benefits their reflection. "Why did I get an 8/10 on my research?" leads to more focused analysis than "Why did I get a 78/100 on this project?"

Use standards instead. A sophisticated extension of the previous tactic, standards-based grading allows teachers to give feedback on an unlimited number of explicit skills. Moreover, that feedback can be given on a non-numerical scale, with students either exceeding, meeting, approaching, or not meeting expectations for any given standard. Math teacher Mark Miles uses this method exclusively in his classes, translating project rubrics into the standards demonstrated and giving regular feedback on work habits and the learning process through standards that reflect the core values and the rubric category ("demonstrate inquiry," "demonstrate process," etc.). Miles translates these standards into a letter grade at the very end of the quarter, but until that point, students are looking at their class performance through the lens of skill descriptions instead of numbers and letters. The standards-based system also allows teachers to provide more personalized feedback by avoiding the pitfalls of the common yardstick. "Maybe exceeding expectations looks different for a student with an IEP than a gifted student," Miles explains. "Their grade may be calculated the same way in the end, but it allows me to differentiate slightly better along the way."

Bury it. If these tactics are too dramatic a shift for your classroom, consider trying something as small as putting the numerical grade at the bottom of the paper instead of the top, or on the back of the page instead of the front, or as a simple number instead of a fractional total (7 versus 7/10). Avoid public announcements about a high or low score, how one class did compared to another, or how students did compared to those from previous years. Let the individual journey take precedence.

For authentic learners, the feedback always matters more than the score. Students always say that the best teachers were the ones who took the time to give them guidance and help them learn—not necessarily the ones they got the best scores from. Give students what they need while they work, and then support their reflective process to match that level of attention.

MAKING THE SHIFT

1. Observe: The next time you hand back an assignment with a numerical grade on it, quietly observe what students do. Who reads the feedback? Who compares grades? Who clearly has a positive reaction? Who clearly has a negative one? How long do they spend looking over the work? Finally, what benefit does this process have for their learning?

2. Imagine: What if you were not only no longer required to give grades, but were actually banned from doing so? How would you provide feedback to your students and help them grow? Apply this imaginary situation to the most frequently recurring assignment that you give in your class. Design the approach, and then ask yourself: What's keeping me from implementing this system right now and making the grade a secondary piece of my feedback? (If there's a good answer to that question, modify your imaginary plan as necessary.)

Integrate student and teacher reflection

This practice has several components. The first is that teacher and student feedback on work should be allowed to live together. If students already engage in peer editing or leave comments for each other on final projects, then there's no reason that this feedback cannot be embraced as a part of the cycle of reflection. Not only does this provide a richer base of feedback for students to base their own reflection on, but it also removes the burden on the teacher of being the sole responder to student work. Teachers can even enter into a dialogue with student commentary, using lines like "I agree with so-and-so's comment on your draft that..." or "I think that so-and-so was actually being too critical of this aspect of your project." This tactic allows teachers to honor student voice while also buffering any feedback that may be off-base. SLA teachers achieve this through a variety of methods: by having audience members and students take notes during a live presentation and then handing back those notes along with their own teacher commentary; by having students read a rough draft and then giving comments—but no grade—via the same rubric that will eventually be used to score the project; by having students participate in a "gallery day" during which they can comment on posted work (on the wall or online) and then incorporating those comments into the final feedback. If student commentary is valued as a part of the assessment process, it will become more authentic—and even carry over to when the feedback isn't linked to the rubric or the grade. Two of the biggest events at SLA each year are the sophomore and freshman science fairs, all-day events where students in one grade level present their work and the rest of the student body serves as audience. Even though the numerical grades for the projects have already been given, the different audiences connect with the presentations based on their position in the process—freshmen are seeking to learn from the sophomores in advance of their own projects, and sophomores later embrace their role as the more experienced students who can really probe into the methods and results of the freshman work. As the freshmen present their lab-report posters, students, teachers, and visiting scientists tour the exhibits together, engaged on the same level.

To further integrate reflection, teachers must open up their own reflection process and allow students in. Unfortunately, the work of teachers and students often remains segregated: the teacher picks the unit and the student completes it; the student takes the test and then the teacher grades it. As a result, the teacher is on a kind of pedagogical island (with a mountain of work to do), and students typically have no concept of that process (and undervalue the work of teachers as a result). With project-based learning, however, the teacher work and student work actually mirror each other: The teacher must come up with an idea, do independent research around it, and present that unit to the class before students can take it up themselves. As a result of that, teachers need to reflect on the curriculum as much as students do, and that means having honest conversations about what's working in the classroom and what should be done differently. This does not mean that students get to question all of the policies and procedures of the class, but it does mean that teachers need to be comfortable with the fact that their curriculum is not monolithic. It is meant to serve the students, and their feedback is essential. This reflection can happen formally, such as via a survey at the end of the unit, or informally, with casual discussions at periodic mile markers. *How is this project going for you? Were the instructions clear? Was the timeline manageable?* This process basically turns that SLA interview question back toward the teacher: If you (the student) were to do this project again, what should I (the teacher) change or do differently?

MAKING THE SHIFT

Review: Take a look at the major projects that one class completes in a school year. For each one, answer the following questions:

- Is there a place for peers to give feedback? *If not, where could you insert one?*
- Does the peer feedback live in the same place as the teacher feedback? *If not, could you combine the two or at least move them closer together?*
- Does the teacher feedback engage with the student feedback? *If not, how could you change the process so that it does?*

Establish norms: Students typically don't have any venue to give their teachers meaningful feedback, and they are accustomed to their suggestions falling on deaf ears. As a result, students might be inclined to present their feedback as complaints or protests instead of something constructive. Change the culture at the very beginning of the year by making it clear that you will be asking for their feedback on a regular basis. Start them on this process early by asking them to report what they need from you, the teacher, and by brainstorming what will make the class productive and successful.

Let reflection accumulate

The practice of letting reflection accumulate supports the meta-cognitive quality of this skill. For many physical tasks, reflection is easy because there's often a clear negative outcome when we're doing things wrong. If we burn enough pieces of toast, we will eventually think to turn down the heat; if we miss enough soccer goals, we will try kicking the ball at a different speed or angle. For most tasks completed in school, though, the abstract nature of the work means that a project (usually) doesn't burst into flame when it wasn't executed well. Even though models may be provided, the success of somebody else's project can be hard to internalize, and students often feel as though they are working in the dark. To know how they are doing, they need feedback from an outside source, usually the teacher. Because this feedback can't happen instantaneously, students are also often delayed in their reflections. This delay threatens to weaken the reflection by preventing it from building on itself. Completed after the work has been done, the reflections aren't immediately useful and therefore may not be internalized as quickly. Also, when reflection has to be extracted from and tacked on to the end of the learning process, students may see it as "just another assignment" instead of a vital component of their growth. One solution is to provide more feedback before the final deadline, so that students have a basis for reflection as they are working. And yet, giving thorough feedback to every student multiple times during a project is an overwhelming prospect for most classroom teachers. Given that end-of-project reflections are the reality, how can they be designed so that students internalize their conclusions?

The answer is that reflection needs to be seen as its own cumulative process, not an end in itself. One easy way to shift to this mindset is by embracing the portfolio model for student work. Presenting the work as pieces that are linked to one another encourages students to see how their own habits and methods are related from one project to the next. Another way is to use a consistent set of questions or prompts for students' reflection, asking them to respond to the rubric criteria or a list of standards (see Appendix G for a list of prompts for reflection). The last way is to organize these reflections so that they remain close to the student and to each other. Whether it's in a single folder, a course module, or an online document, this proximity reminds students that reflection is a process and encourages their subsequent commentary to build on what they have already said.

At SLA, teachers use these different approaches in a variety of combinations. Several of them are implemented in the 11th grade, when students are writing their analytical "2Fer essays" (described at the start of Chapter 2). Their online documents are required to contain a rough draft with comments made by a peer editor, a final draft with comments made by the teacher, and lastly their own reflection, where they must comment on the five rubric categories for the assignment. The box prompts them to "take notes in each category about what worked well and what you need to improve." This activity must be completed before they can start their next paper, which begins right below the reflection, on the same document. These reflections also serve as source material for their "self-reflective 2Fer essays," in which students must analyze a pattern in their own writing at the middle and end of the year. By the time they are writing the final paper, students may not have conquered the weak spots in their writing, but at the very least they know what those weaknesses are and can identify when they happen. As a result, students are well on their way to resolving those issues as they write instead of relying on the teacher to tell them what they did right or wrong. By letting these reflections become more than the sum of their parts, eventually students will internalize these areas for improvement and implement them as they are working with that particular skill, not just after the fact.

MAKING THE SHIFT

Evaluate: What skills do students use repeatedly over the year? Make as complete a list as you can, and then pick the 5–10 skills that you see as in greatest need of improvement—these are where students need to work on their metacognitive reflection. Then make a second list: In which assignments do these skills

---

MAKING THE SHIFT—*(continued)*

appear? You now have the chain of work that students should also see as connected, so that their reflections on each assignment build on the previous one.

Standardize: What do you use to give feedback to your students on their work? Collect any rubrics, checklists, questionnaires, or other mediums. These formats should also be what students use to guide their reflections—keeping the language consistent will help their observations stick. (If you are using a different set of criteria for every single assignment, consider how you could unify your own process, as well.)

Roadblocks and Work-arounds

Teacher: "How do you grade reflection?" This is where the spirit of reflection—thinking for the sake of improving your own learning—bumps up against the reality of classroom routine. Reflection can be counted as a part of the "process" grade on SLA's schoolwide rubric. So how do you assess it meaningfully?

Look for active steps toward a solution. It's easy for students to point out their weak spots, but it takes more effort to actually improve those skills. Require students to begin to solve their issues. If they avoid showing their work on a problem set, require that they successfully chart all of their steps at least once. If they struggle with providing sufficient context and credentials for a source, require that they go back and look it up. Linking their reflection to an explicit task gets them in the metacognitive habit—and also gives you something concrete to grade.

Hold the final product to the standards of an earlier reflection. If students only complete their reflections after the fact, they're not as likely to see the value in their conclusions. By putting reflection first, students get a chance to set their own criteria for what success looks like. For the next project, include an item in the checklist or rubric that assesses how successful students were at improving their own weak spot. By personalizing their process, students have increased ownership of the project and a clearer roadmap of how to improve.

Just don't grade it. The previous two suggestions are designed to use grades as a kind of carrot to actually lead students *away* from thinking about grades as the definitive commentary on their work. If your students are already invested in their own reflective practice, by all means, don't feel the need to slap a grade on their good thinking!

Student: "My reflection showed me that I'm disorganized/I procrastinated/I had other work to do." There are many reasons that a project manages to meet or fall short of expectations, and the process of creation is a big one (which is why SLA includes it as a category in the schoolwide rubric). As a result, this kind of reflection on work habits is common and necessary. Students need to reflect on the ups and downs of their path, especially if the work isn't getting finished on time, or at all. However, students also need to be coached not to let this reflection on process be the *only* thing that they think about, because it crowds out a deeper reflection about the status of their skills. If all they reflect on is how they waited to write the paper at the last minute, they're not paying any attention to their ability to write transitions or provide context for quotes. Giving students an open-ended prompt like "How did you do on this project?" potentially leaves them room for these sorts of generalizations. To encourage more specific thinking, provide an explicit spot for reflections about process, but make the majority of the prompts about specific skills.

Student: "It's my group's fault that I didn't do a good job." The group project can run into similar difficulties when students are reflecting after the deadline. Reflection on collaboration is essential, but students are sometimes tempted to hang their own weaknesses on a partner's shortcomings. The contracts and daily goal setting described earlier in the chapter can go a long way in preventing this kind of behavior, but so can adjustments to reflections at the end of the project. Instead of asking students to report on their own performance, make them responsible for reporting about the skills of everybody else in the group. Discuss with the class that this is a reciprocal process: "You will be giving feedback to your peers to assist their growth, and you have to trust that they will give you commentary with your own best interests in mind." Even the most acrimonious of groups will reflect carefully when they know that their partners are doing the same for them. Making this reflection a part of the final grade places even more value (and positive pressure) on group members to keep their criticism constructive.

Modeling Reflection Schoolwide

Reflection can be a challenge to implement on a larger scale because people often approach it with the "one more thing" mindset, as in "that's one more thing we don't have time for." Instead of trying to add the practice to an already crammed daily and yearly schedule, reflection can be injected into already existing practices with excellent results.

The biggest way that SLA incorporates reflection into the school-wide routine is with report card conferences. In many schools, these conferences are done open-house style, with parents standing in long lines to talk to certain teachers, but overall attendance is poor. At SLA, the situation is flipped. Families make an appointment to meet with one person—their child's advisor—and attendance is high, with the expectation that every conference will be completed, if not in person, then by phone.

The centerpiece of these conferences is the narrative report card. Twice a year teachers write a short description of each child's performance in their class, which is accompanied by a description of that quarter's coursework and reporting about standards-based grades. Teachers know their students well, and sometimes the most insightful advice or commentary they could provide can't be communicated through a traditional report card. Admittedly, this task *does* add to the workload of teachers, as writing the narratives takes longer than just typing in a number grade. The practice pays off, however, in how the students interact with the narratives. They first read them during the advisory period, when they have time to read, digest, respond, and prepare for their report card conferences. During the conference, they then have a conversation with both their advisor and their family about their academic performance. Because everyone present has access to the insight of half a dozen teachers, the conference can focus on solutions and best practices instead of just an interrogation about how things are going and why. Because students stay with the same advisory for their entire high school career, they also benefit from the cumulative knowledge that their advisor collects over the years (more on that relationship in Chapter 7, "Embracing the Culture.")

The narrative report card process encourages the adults involved to value student voice. Many advisors have their advisees lead the conference, giving them a chance to take ownership of their academic successes and failures (and thereby preempting their parents' possible negative reaction if the report card is a disappointment). Many teachers also give students some kind of survey in advance of writing the narratives. In the study skills support class, learning specialist Beth Menasion asks students "to reflect on their executive functioning, study skills, and metacognition." Menasion incorporates their reflection into her own narrative, adding her commentary in response. Senior teachers take it a step further when, for the very last conference of their high school career, students are asked to write their own narrative from scratch. Teachers review the write-ups and also add their commentary if they think the student has overlooked something.

All of these practices transform report cards from a monolithic reckoning to a productive conversation. The experience gives students invaluable practice in the art of presenting themselves to others, whether it's describing their work habits during a job interview or providing salient details to a teacher who is going to write them a letter of recommendation.

Back to the Beginning

Now that you are at the end of this chapter, hopefully the title "Making Reflection Relevant" makes more sense. Too often, reflection is pigeonholed as a just-sit-there practice, something that young people aren't inclined to do or don't know how to do well. If that's true, then it's because of the way adults force reflection upon them—either as punishment ("Go to your room and think about what you've done!")

or unwanted intrusion ("What's on your mind these days?"). Reflection needs to be reframed as both intrinsic and valuable—the secret tool that can help them conquer the challenges of their academic life, and beyond.

STUDENT PERSPECTIVE: REFLECTION

Tucker Bartholomew, Class of 2013

When I left SLA I was confident in my ability to perform, and believed that my first semester – which included a biology class and a two-part economics course – would go smoothly. I was wrong. It turns out I was unprepared for my newfound freedom outside of the classroom. To put it simply, I did not know how to allot my time.

Thankfully, reflection helped me overcome my quickly forming bad habit of wasted hours. A week before I went into finals, I took time to think about how I spent my regular day. It did not take me long to realize that I could be doing a lot better in my classes if I just made a few changes to my daily routine. Over the next week, I exercised in the morning, studied throughout the day, and somehow made it to bed before 11 PM every night. I felt healthier, more active in my classes, and most importantly I felt more prepared for finals week. By reviewing myself, I was actually able to change habits for the better.

In my second semester at school, reflection has been playing a big role in my course work as well. Currently I am enrolled in an introductory course called "We Are Our Own Devils," which focuses on writing about how we have seen or experienced pain. This is actually reflection in and of itself; however, what is so humorously coincidental is the assignment that comes after the papers: the post write-up. A post write-up is quintessentially everything I was instructed to do in high school. I analyze my final draft of my paper after submission, look for areas I believe could have been improved, and then I submit a 1-2 page paper to my professor that details my official reflection on my own work.

7 | Embracing the Culture: Schoolwide Practices

Now that you have read about the core values of this framework, you hopefully are thinking about ways to implement it on your own. However, you might also be experiencing some trepidation about making the shift. Can students really take ownership of their work to this degree? Can I manage my classroom successfully while still allowing for messy collaboration? What needs to be in place before I start teaching for all this to function?

You are experiencing the common reactions that SLA visitors go through when they come to our school. When they see our model in action, many educators are incredibly enthusiastic about the work that we do. They appreciate how comfortable and friendly everybody seems to be. They are humbled by the ability of students to speak about the school as a whole. They fawn over the projects that students are creating during class time. (With several hundred visitors a year, students are pleasantly unfazed by this extra attention.)

This initial enthusiasm then transitions into a phase of intensive questioning. *How do you get the students to be like this? What's unique or different about this school? How did you create this culture? Does it all stem from the classroom, or does it appear from other places as well?* The answer to that last question is yes, there are other practices and policies in place that help support this particular culture of teaching and learning. This chapter is all about them. Each section will describe a different key facet of school culture, from common language to unique programs.

Of course, the very presence of these schoolwide practices sometimes deflates the enthusiasm of visitors. They become convinced that without being able to replicate all of these exact practices at their school, there's no way they could shift the culture of teaching and learning. Sometimes visitors even use this as validation for skepticism they already had—that SLA couldn't possibly be re-created somewhere else.

The funny thing is, we kind of agree with those skeptics. The school where this model was developed is indeed unique and can't be replicated. But why would anybody want that? Educator (and repeat visitor to SLA) Bud Hunt put it well after witnessing a batch of visitors express their love for the model and then dismiss its viability elsewhere:

> Of course your school won't be like theirs. You aren't in downtown Philadelphia. You don't operate in the same space. Your families are different. So, for that matter, are you.

SLA is experiencing this process itself with the founding of its second campus, SLA@Beeber. Even though we do most of the same things, the school has developed its own version of the culture, reflective of its staff, students, location, and extended community. The beauty of a strong framework is that it's expansive instead of limiting.

In that spirit, this chapter seeks to help you understand the pieces of the model that don't appear directly in the core values. Those pieces have been boiled down to five categories: *common language*, *open doors*, *outside partnerships*, *advisory*, and *first days*. In the sections that follow, I describe each of these with an overview and then provide an analysis of the essential benefits. Lastly, I provide suggestions on how to "scale it down" for teachers who are looking to bring these benefits to their individual practice. My SLA colleagues and I recognize that when it comes to changing the culture, the more staff on board, the better—but we also believe in the incredible power a single educator has to transform his or her own classroom.

Common Language

Visitors to SLA frequently comment that the students here really know what they're talking about—and by this they mean more than just that our kids are capable or smart. The language our students use reveals a real engagement with the pedagogy of the school—so much so that teachers are quite comfortable handing visitor questions about teaching and learning directly over to them. This understanding goes beyond a few key phrases. The way that SLA talks about teaching and learning reflects a thorough, common vision, and it touches many different pieces of the school. Instead of slogans or mantras, the concepts that SLA employs are flexible and can be applied across different disciplines and situations. Teachers use the common language so naturally that students absorb it automatically; indeed, the practice feels invisible until an outsider comments on how unusual it is. Here are a few categories of the common language that matter most:

The core values

After the last five chapters, this category may seem obvious—but the importance of explicitly communicating these five concepts to students cannot be underestimated. They are listed on big posters displayed around the school: Inquiry, Research, Collaboration, Presentation, Reflection. The values give students a way to talk about their learning that goes beyond the vague description of "we learned it." Instead, students can use the values to build descriptions of the work, starting with "We learned by..."

The rubric

You may have already checked it out, but as a reminder, the SLA rubric (Appendix A) has five categories that stay the same across disciplines: Design, Knowledge, Application, Presentation, and Process. These terms turn into a common vocabulary that teachers use to talk to students about their learning. As a result, statements such as "you design great projects, but you're disorganized about your process" or "you had a great presentation, but your core knowledge of the material was not demonstrated in the final product" could be made by teachers in any discipline, and such statements are more likely to resonate with students if they are hearing similar language across disciplines and over time.

Standards by discipline

As discussed in Chapter 6, standards-based grading allows teachers to create language that is common to their own discipline. This language can be adopted or adapted from local or national standards; professional groups for different disciplines also often have suggested lists of essential skills and knowledge. These standards provide students with a concrete answer to the question "What am I expected to learn in this class?" Ideally, the standards language also helps unify those expectations across a grade level or even for the sequence of courses over multiple years. The math department has four standards that stay the same for each course, plus content-specific knowledge standards specific to each class. By contrast, the history department has five categories of standards, with the specific expectations becoming more rigorous with each passing year. As described by their department write-up, this upward spiral of learning has a clear set of outcomes: "By graduation, the goal is for students to develop the ability to effectively analyze primary source documents, research independently, express the impact of perspective and bias in history, meaningfully contribute to classroom discussions, and evaluate the connections between the modern world and history." With the standards language embedded in the coursework, this detailed description is not a lofty fantasy; it's a logical outcome of a carefully constructed sequence. (See Appendix H for SLA's current iteration of standards by discipline.)

School rules

SLA has three rules:

1. Respect yourself.
2. Respect the community.
3. Respect SLA as a place of learning.

Occasionally these rules get referred to as "guidelines," which is probably a more accurate way to describe them, except that the shift in terminology encourages students to say, "There are no rules at this school," which is not true. What there *aren't* at SLA are big lists of "do not's," along with warnings about punishments and repercussions. In fact, apart from the district-wide policies about serious disciplinary infractions, the school has only two pre-defined situations in which the "if you do *x*, you will receive *y* punishment" applies: being late to school and riding the elevator without a pass.

For students coming out of stricter learning environments, this guidelines-based approach to behavior can take some adjustment. The good news is, it's a shift that asks them to take ownership of their actions—and when they do, it means that they also own their learning. How is this achieved? Through a lot of discussion, and that discussion needs to start well before something goes wrong. The question "What does respect look like?" asks students to set expectations for themselves with their response. Instead of creating a laundry list of rules that anticipate the potential (and therefore inevitable) wrongdoing of the student body, our three guidelines ask students to identify and commit to responsible behavior.

Essential benefits

Common language encourages a focus on learning over grades. Note that none of the common language described here relies on the vague descriptors usually associated with achievement, such as "excellence" or "mastery." Even on the rubric, which does have space for a number grade, the different levels refer to whether students are exceeding, meeting, approaching, or not meeting expectations. And students are quite aware that "expectations" may look different from one pupil to the next. When they have all of the other common language to discuss their learning process, this approach feels natural: everybody's learning process is unique, and we need the vocabulary to describe our differences.

Common language empowers students. Many schools fall into the trap of creating a useful language of teaching and learning for staff and then keeping it a complete secret from the children. The result is a strange hierarchy that denies students any agency in their own learning process by making them the object of their learning instead of the master of it. Talking with students explicitly about curriculum and pedagogy shows them that they deserve a voice in this conversation. When that happens, not only does the quality of their education improve, but they begin to see that they have the ability to talk knowledgably with adults on any number of topics—and the right to do so, as well.

Common language helps teachers support each other. Creating a thoughtful, caring, empowered culture in your individual class can be exhausting. Likewise, for students, figuring out the different policies and procedures for a half dozen different classes and teachers can be punishing. Although adopting common language takes extra time at the outset, the ongoing payoff is that the values you care about are being reinforced during the entire school day. When math and English teachers both evaluate students for their "application" and "process" of solving a problem or analyzing a poem, their content areas no longer seem so diametrically opposed. Likewise, using the same guidelines to discuss student behavior communicates to students that you are devoted to their individual growth, instead of just maintaining order within the confines of your room.

SCALE IT DOWN

Within a school: Print and compare everything that you hand out to students during the first days of school: course policies and procedures, syllabi, letters home, and classroom rules. Put yourself in your students' shoes: What is essential here? What could be streamlined or combined? What are they likely to flat-out ignore? How could common language make the expectations for each class easier to understand?

SCALE IT DOWN—*(continued)*

Within a discipline: Write a "scope and sequence" document. Have teachers in your discipline brainstorm what knowledge and skills they expect students to have when they finish the course sequence. Combine your brainstorms into one list, and then backwards-map what steps students take during each year of their studies to get there. You now have a list of standards for your discipline! Even if these do not become a part of the grading routine, they can be posted in classrooms and used as a framework for talking with students about their work.

Within a classroom: Instead of pushing a list of rules onto students, have them brainstorm what guidelines will work for the class. Use the three SLA rules (or another short set of guidelines) as a conversation starter, and examples of what these guidelines look like in action, adding items if necessary. Consolidate the list, if necessary, and then post it prominently in the room. When students aren't following their own examples, encourage them to respectfully police each other and help get the class back on track.

Within a classroom: Identify what essential skills students are using throughout the year, and create categories for a rubric that reflects those skills. Challenge yourself to align all of your major assigments to this new rubric. Let students know from day one that your expectations for their work span the year.

Open Doors

For many teachers, the idea of an open-door policy for their classroom is terrifying—because the only people they expect to walk through that door are going to evaluate (aka criticize) their practice. A few years ago in Philadelphia, a 3rd grade teacher had her classroom reading corner dismantled and removed by district walk-through inspectors because they decided it was "clutter." (Luckily, the press got hold of the story, and the furniture was eventually returned.) Incidents like these make educators feel like they have to keep their door closed just to protect the good things in their classrooms from being destroyed.

This practice—though often justified—often has the unintended side effect of encouraging a closed-door mindset. Teachers spend the overwhelming majority of their workday alone with their students, and free moments in the school day are mostly used to depressurize, catch up on grading, or set up for the next lesson. This routine can quickly turn into a kind of vacuum, where neither the teacher nor the students have any contact with anyone outside the class.

An inquiry-based curriculum challenges this kind of attitude, and the Internet helps students push down classroom walls with ease. However, the ease of connectivity over the web can highlight the lack of connection within a school building. As Google global education evangelist Jaime Casap put it during a panel discussion at EduCon, "Why are students in 205 connecting with kids halfway around the world when they don't even have a relationship with the kids in 207?" Here are some ways that open doors in your school can help support personalized inquiry in your classroom.

Shared planning. Many schools have a subset of teachers who are reluctant to share their curriculum or lesson plans. Sometimes this reluctance comes out of a sense of ownership: I made this, and therefore it belongs to me. A true inquiry-based curriculum, however, doesn't really belong to the teacher; instead, it sets the stage for the student to create something unique. As a result, teachers devoted to inquiry are always searching for the best vehicle for their students' advancement. SLA teachers post all of their units online and can share them at will with other staff members. They also have two hours of common planning time a week, which are periodically dedicated to lesson planning.

Direct conversations. When students are pursuing their own line of inquiry, they are likely to need guidance or resources beyond what their classroom teacher can provide. Conveniently, the entire school can be used as a source of knowledge, populated with student and teacher experts. Peer editing and "speed learning" (described in

Chapter 5) are two ways that students engage in these direct conversations within the classroom; expanding these practices to encompass the whole school enriches the culture of learning immensely. SLA has both a math lab and a literacy lab (staffed by teachers and hand-picked student tutors during our long lunch periods) that provide one-on-one support for those skills. Students also connect with their former teachers for feedback on a project or advice on where to apply to college. These conversations don't have to happen in person, either. As long as students know that the channel of communication is open, they will use it. I recently provided translation services for a student I don't even teach. He was researching the Holocaust, found a document he couldn't read, and his teacher referred him to me because he knew that I could translate it from the German. In a quick e-mail exchange, I was able to provide a useful service and support another student's learning.

Classroom visitors. One of my favorite things about SLA is that nobody is fazed when a visitor comes into a classroom. Whether it's another teacher, the principal, or even somebody students have never seen before, students are generally unfazed by the presence of somebody who isn't normally there. The same goes for teachers. When you are only having one or two formal observations a year, visitors are a cause of anxiety. But when your door is open to many people, those visits can become a source of strength for your classroom A cornerstone of this practice is EduCon, our annual education conference that attracts hundreds of guests interested in the intersection of education and technology. They spend a Friday visiting school while it is in session, which jump-starts the conversations that happen at the sessions that weekend. Teachers relish the opportunity to share and unpack their practice with like-minded educators from across the country.

In addition to these outside observers, SLA has a system of professional learning communities that connects teachers across disciplines to observe each other's work and provide neutral feedback. Because teachers are not necessarily experts in another subject area, their commentary seeks to reflect on the use of inquiry and the student experience in the class instead of nitpicking the details of the content presented. (That is not to say that teachers of the same subject don't visit each other. Subject area teachers have common planning time, so they seek inspiration and feedback from each other on a regular basis as well.)

Student Assistant Teachers (SATs). This program places SLA seniors in underclass courses to provide general learning support for younger students. SATs attend their selected class full time and receive academic credit for their work. More important, they have active relationships with their teacher mentors, meeting on a regular basis to plan out what they will be doing in the class and to reflect on how the work is going. Their presence provides a bridge between grades, giving underclassmen a role model to look up to and the seniors a meaningful reason to stay engaged as graduation nears. Moreover, their responsibilities are not superficial—whether it's providing individual help, teaching mini-lessons, or managing classroom administration, SLA teachers rely on these seniors to enrich the learning environment for everybody involved.

Essential benefits

Open doors enrich the culture of learning. When educators are willing to talk one-on-one about learning, it affirms that what the students are up to is worthwhile. Teachers' involvement shows that they also think of their work as more than just a job. These factors encourage students to keep talking about what they're doing after the bell rings.

Open doors save teachers time. The workload of both preparing and implementing inquiry-based curriculum can be crushing. By sharing content or writing units collaboratively, teachers can both strengthen their work and save valuable time and energy. By letting assistants into the room, it takes the pressure off of the teacher to be the sole manager of classroom administration and culture. And by letting colleagues observe and give constructive criticism, teachers can fine-tune their teaching sooner rather than later, and that's good for students as well as for the teachers' own formal observations.

SCALE IT DOWN

Within a discipline: If subject teachers have no experience collaborating or sharing with each other, start small. Share one unit, schedule one cross-visit, agree to adopt one common assignment. A great place to start is by comparing course syllabi and any policies and procedures; it's often eye-opening for teachers to see the wide range of expectations and styles that students are confronted with from their many different instructors.

Within a classroom: Create one assignment in which students must connect with a source outside the classroom but inside the school to complete. They might need to search for an expert on a particular topic, or maybe present themselves as the experts, surveying or interviewing younger students. (If you're going to have students seek input from teachers exclusively, make sure to give your colleagues advance warning.) When the project finishes, arrange for time to share the results with the "outsiders" the class engaged with.

Outside Partnerships

The practice of outside partnerships is a natural extension of having open doors—once people are connecting with each other within a school, the logical next step is to collaborate with experts outside the building. This practice has already been described on the classroom level in Chapter 4. This section describes some of the ways that outside partnership is embedded across grade levels.

At SLA, outside partnership is at the very core of the school; we have a partner institution in the Franklin Institute, the nation's oldest science museum. From hosting our freshmen for special programming on Wednesday afternoons to providing scholarships to seniors pursuing careers in STEM, this partnership touches many points of an SLA student's life and is an inextricable part of the school's identity.

Apart from this big connection, many partnerships for students happen on an individual basis. Wednesday afternoons are reserved for this work—in-school instruction ends at 1 p.m. and students then head out to different programming depending on their grade level (while teachers have common planning time). Freshmen are at the museum, but sophomores and juniors participate in their own internship, called individualized learning programs (ILP). These placements are reflective of a student's own interests. At the beginning of the year, students can browse a large directory of already established partnerships or seek to set up their own. Students connect with institutions all over the city, from law firms and hospitals to elementary schools and even the local zoo. They attend their internship for two hours a week. For some, the placement turns into a two-year position, or even a paid summer job. ILPs give many students their first taste of life out in the working world—and the responsibilities that come with it.

These two years "in the field" help prepare students for their culminating work at SLA—the senior capstone project. Instead of having an ILP, seniors use their two hours a week to conceive, design, and execute a comprehensive, multidisciplinary project that is the culmination of their learning at SLA. This project also requires that they find an outside mentor to guide them in their work. This mentor can be a classroom teacher, but in many cases it is a working expert in the field that they are exploring. Sometimes this mentorship grows directly out of an ILP experience; at other times students cultivate it on their own or make a connection via the professional networks of the school's teachers and their families. Capstone program manager (and physics teacher) Roz Echols maximizes this network by having teachers brainstorm all of the potential mentors they know and putting their names into a common database. When students are stuck finding someone to work with them, she can search the list to see if the school might already have a suitable mentor on call. These partnerships don't have to happen in person, but they do involve regular contact and sharing of work. At the end of the year, seniors present their work as both a graduation requirement and as a celebration of all they have achieved at the school. Whether it's writing a novel, building a robot, founding a community service program, or putting on a fashion show, the community turns out to appreciate the project of each individual student—the outcome of four years of project-based learning.

Essential benefits

Outside partnerships extend learning into the real world. A fruitful outside partnership should not just support the student in achieving a school-specific goal. Instead, it should push that student's learning past school walls, past the end of the day, and possibly even past graduation. The regimented nature of modern schools does a frightfully poor job of showing students what it's like to actually work in a particular field (apart from, of course, becoming a teacher). Outside partnerships give them that crucial window. The worst outcome—that students realize a particular type of work isn't for them—is still a very valuable one!

Outside partnerships supplement teacher knowledge. A recurring challenge addressed in this book is how the classroom teacher can support students as they pursue their own personalized lines of inquiry. This approach toward learning never assumes that the classroom teacher can be the sole "expert" for such a rich diversity of student projects. When students are really pursuing what interests them, outside partnerships become an essential support for everyone involved with the learning process. By encouraging students to go directly to the field that interests them, teachers can position themselves as advisors instead of gatekeepers, providing guidance for the logistics of the project and coaching students on how to interact professionally with the outside partner.

SCALE IT DOWN

Within a discipline: Brainstorm which professions are the end result of studying your subject. Students should have working partnerships with adults in these fields, connections that go beyond a "career day" or a class visit. What projects are they completing that would benefit from outside mentorship? These

SCALE IT DOWN—*(continued)*

kinds of programs can be easier to implement with older grades; if the partnership can't be extended down, let older students present their work to the younger grades as a preview of the opportunities available in the future.

Within a classroom: A typical school schedule does not make time for two hours of outside internship a week, but this type of program can still be implemented over the course of a year. Once a list of partners has been developed (with the help of teachers, students, and their families), students could visit their placement quarterly or monthly and report back to the class as a part of their grade. Alternately, the entire class could participate in an ongoing partnership with one group, making periodic site visits and also welcoming guests into the class.

Advisory

Advisory is the program that principal Chris Lehmann refers to as "the soul of the school." Instead of having a brief homeroom period five days a week, SLA has a longer advisory period twice a week. This time is used to fill out the curriculum and meet the larger social, emotional, and academic needs of the students, as well as take care of any administrative tasks that don't fit into the rest of the school day.

A general four-year sequence determines what gets done in each quarter in advisory, and it reflects the changing position of the advisees from one year to the next. Freshman year is largely occupied with helping students get to know each other, and they often do a mini-presentation sharing a personal interest or skill. It's also time to introduce the many policies and procedures of the school, get students acclimated to their laptops, and shore up their academic and organizational skills. Sophomore year encourages students to start thinking about the bigger picture, researching an issue of importance to teens, completing community service, and learning about the college application process. Junior year starts the college process in earnest, and senior year is dominated by both the college process and managing capstone projects.

When I asked teachers to describe what advisory is used for, several of them responded with, "What *isn't* it used for?" They meant this in a good way. In the face of increasingly rigid state and national standards around curriculum, advisory time makes space to meet the needs of the students as they arise. SLA has a database of relevant advisory lesson plans, and advisory cohorts meet periodically to discuss what they would like the entire grade to achieve during that quarter (with guidance from the advisors whose students are a year older). However, advisories have flexibility to address something in the news or an event at school that students wish to discuss. Moreover, individual advisors also have control over what gets done any particular period. They might postpone a plan if students are in crisis, request a work period, or just really need to play a cooperative game and enjoy their advisor's company.

Embedded in this advisory time is the relationship of the advisors to their students, as well as the relationships of the students to each other. Everybody is in the same "advisory family" for all four years of their time at SLA. They meet each other before the first day of freshman year, and their advisor is on stage to greet them when they are handed their diploma at graduation. In the intervening time, the advisor serves as the point person for that student and the student's family. Advisors schedule and facilitate report card conferences, attend any administrative or disciplinary meetings, and write the counselor letter of recommendation when it's time to apply to college. Students can trust that the advisor will be their devoted advocate at the school, no matter what is going on with them personally or academically. Similarly, students come to love and trust their fellow advisees in a relationship that goes way beyond the camaraderie of an academic classroom. Advisees are asked to support each other from day one, starting by checking in about upcoming assignments and making sure everybody is on top of their work. This focus expands to supporting each other through all of life's ups and downs. An advisory will cheer someone on when they get into their dream college; embrace them when they come out as LGBT; console them and attend the funeral when a family member passes away. Students cannot check their lives at the door when they enter school; advisory becomes a place where life can be both dealt with and celebrated.

Essential benefits

Advisory provides continuity. Having one teacher as the point person for a student's entire school career allows for a truly deep relationship and understanding. Advisors quickly learn a student's strengths and weaknesses, the ins and outs of the family situation, and any other relevant quirks or details. This knowledge can help keep things running smoothly both in the classroom and in the student's life outside of school. If a student is floundering in class, that teacher can go right to the advisor and seek guidance: Is this new, or is it a pattern? What intervention works well? What should be avoided? A teacher may conference with a student and also contact the family directly, but the advisor is always there to follow up and reinforce the message (whether it's one praising the student or encouraging improvement). The advisor then carries that knowledge into the next school year, and can pass it along to new teachers.

Advisory provides balance. As discussed previously, advisors have the autonomy to put the needs of their students above the set lesson for any given day (with the understanding that they'll get to the original plan eventually). Students may have been seeking to meet the demands of their teachers all day, but they know that advisory is a time when *their* own needs will be met. This kind of reciprocity helps create balance in a pretty demanding academic environment.

SCALE IT DOWN

In a classroom: There are a number of ways to build in the kind of connection that advisors have with their students, but they involve reserving a bit of time that should be free of strictly academic pursuits. At the start of the year, have students

SCALE IT DOWN—*(continued)*

complete a personal survey that asks them to share relevant information about themselves: their strengths and weaknesses in that subject, sure, but also unexpected information, like what their passion is outside of class, and what you can't tell just by looking at them. These prompts may even turn into inspiration for projects, but at first they are a way to honor each other as people.

In a department: Institutional knowledge about students often gets shared in dribs and drabs, with teachers praising students who wow them and groaning about students who chronically underperform. Teachers can get a more complete picture of their students from one year to the next if they do a quick catalog of student traits. These notes could be subject-specific, relate to general academic and metacognitive skills, or just provide tips and tricks for having a productive relationship with that student. To avoid bias, the inventories should not be value judgments— just a snapshot of must-know information for a teacher who is otherwise going in blind.

First Days

Two weeks before the first day of school, SLA freshmen show up for the Summer Institute program. For three days, the students participate in a variety of activities designed to preview both the curriculum and the culture of SLA in a low-pressure environment.

The programming runs for the morning only and is divided into three sections. First, the entire grade is greeted and plays some kind of get-to-know-you or cooperative game. Then the students are split into their advisory groups and spend time getting to know what will be their school family for the next four years. Here the advisors have the opportunity to bond with their advisees before the grind of the school year begins. They often play more games, talk about school expectations, and bring in now-graduated former advisees to provide a student perspective.

The last part of the day belongs to the expedition groups, and this becomes the dominant activity by the end of the week. These groups are tasked with exploring a nearby area of the city and pursuing a line of inquiry in that area. What this looks like in practice varies widely from group to group and year to year. Locations are all within walking distance and include nearby parks, the riverfront, an indoor shopping center, and the regional train station. Students develop questions relating to any number of categories: nature, social interaction, architecture, commerce, or infrastructure, to name a few. Once they identify their question, they have a day to collect information to help answer their question. Usually these research sessions involve time out in the field, observing, surveying, or measuring; straight-up historical queries can involve consulting online or print resources, but the majority of inquiry tries to make sense of the world as it is happening.

At the end of the institute, the group must package their findings and then present their inquiry project to the rest of the grade, thus completing their introduction to each other and the five core values as well.

Essential benefits

Summer Institute puts learning first. Making space for an introductory orientation allows students to engage with the core values without the extrinsic pressure of grades. Meeting in August gives the program a bit of a summer camp atmosphere. Sessions meet in classrooms, but the school is otherwise empty, and the activities feel fresh, unencumbered by the routines and policies of the school year. From the instructional end, the teacher-facilitators don't have to worry about communicating specific expectations, composing a rubric, or assessing students on their work. Instead, they can focus on helping students develop their prowess with the five core values. With each new step of the expedition, teachers help students brainstorm around the value: What makes a good question? What information do we need to answer that question? How are we going to get it? How will we then present that information in a way that makes other people care about our findings? Come September, teachers of freshmen can refer back to this work when introducing a more complex project for the first time.

Summer Institute puts students before teachers. As with most programming at SLA, the students drive this work, not the teachers. Not only is the mini-course designed to honor student inquiry; the institute itself relies heavily on volunteer assistants from the current student body as well as graduates. Each teacher is assigned one or more upperclassmen to help out with the expedition groups, and these volunteers usually take the lead when it comes to explaining the core values, just as graduates are tapped by their former advisors to give advice to the incoming freshmen. In its design, the message is clear: this school belongs to you.

SCALE IT DOWN

In a classroom: Hosting a program before the school year begins may not be possible, but the same clean slate exists during the first few days of school. Postpone the administrative minutiae in favor of letting kids explore and practice the skills that will be essential to the course, no grades attached. Don't be afraid to let the days feel like something different. Getting students out of their academic routine will help them shake off their school persona (high-achieving and anxious about grades, middle-of-the-road and not trying to impress anybody, or sick of school and not afraid to let it show) and get down to the authentic business of learning.

In a classroom: Whenever possible, loop in former students to aid with classroom work. This can include graduates who might have college or work schedules that are flexible enough to allow them to come visit, or upperclassmen who have a free period or can be "borrowed" from another class for a bit. Invite them at the beginning of the year to give insight to your classroom culture, in the middle of projects to describe how they did the work and what they would have done differently, or anytime at all to serve as models for what you can do with the knowledge in later classes, in college, in life.

Moving Forward

Congratulations! You've now gotten a full picture of SLA's teaching and learning in the digital age. I hope you have enjoyed getting to see a few slices from that journey, especially in this last chapter. More important, I hope that you see a path for your own classroom, department, and school. As I did at the beginning of this chapter, I'll leave you with the thoughts of Bud Hunt on this matter:

> [SLA] staff built a place that made sense as a combination of the places they came from, the places they were, and the places and ideas that they wanted to build with. *They* made the place. Together. With their students. And you can make a place, too. But it'll be different, deliciously, brilliantly different... because good schools are about context and environment and about taking what you have and what you want and striking a balance and working very, very hard. Good schools are about people honestly and intentionally working together very purposefully.

Hopefully this text helps you continue that honest, intentional work in your own environment and helps you find ways to make learning authentic for your own students.

STUDENT PERSPECTIVE: ADVISORY

Ryan Harris, Class of 2013

In our first year together, I honestly have to say that my advisory did not bond. Being a naturally quiet person myself, I tended to keep to myself and not engage with anybody. We would come and go like it was any other class, and stick with our own friends.

For a while, that worked just fine. But starting at the end of freshman year, Mr. Herman seemed to have had enough with our apathetic attitude toward advisory and felt a change was due. One big change was something simple: birthdays. Whenever somebody's birthday was approaching, we'd make a total day of it during advisory. We'd always do things like sing "Happy Birthday" to each other—sometimes in the most obnoxious, but funny, way. Through something as simple as birthday parties, we became closer with one another. Advisory became a time to have fun and hang out. I got to open up more with my fellow advisees.

While we may not have become best friends with one another, the clique mentality more or less dissolved within our little community. As the years went on, we developed our little "family" of sorts. And as all families do, we developed our own little traditions. One tradition was putting on an event for Halloween. One year, we all dressed up as zombies and went around scaring the other advisories. We did our own makeup, organizing, and even kept it a secret from all the other students. I'm not sure we succeeded in actually scaring anybody, but it was an awesome bonding experience for all of us. It demonstrated that advisory wasn't just something that was taken for granted, but rather a place where strong bonds and great memories can be formed.

Appendix A
School Project Rubric

SLA Standard Rubric

	Design 20	Knowledge 20	Application 20	Presentation 20	Process 20
Exceeds Expectations 20–19					
Meets Expectations 18–15					
Approaches Expectations 14–13					
Does Not Meet Expectations 12–0					
Totals					

Appendix B
SLA's Acceptable Use Policy

Science Leadership Academy values technology and encourages its use in creative ways to support student learning in a safe and secure learning environment. This policy is a guide to ensuring the appropriate use as well as safety for all community members. While these technologies provide powerful learning opportunities, they must be used responsibly.

These rules apply to any electronic device including laptops, mobile phones, MP3 players, gaming devices, digital cameras, any and all devices that are connected to the School District of Philadelphia network. Learning always takes priority while using SLA's wireless and hardwired Internet connections.

Trespassing

- Do not touch another person's laptop/device unless invited by the owner.
- Do not play with, use, or change another person's user account.
- Do not access another person's files or resources.
- Only access areas of the network you have been given permission to access.

No Fooling Around

- Do not load any game, video, or music file on your machine that is not paid for or that you do not have the rights to use.
- Do not play games at school, unless sanctioned and agreed to by staff and parents.
- Do not access inappropriate websites (obscene, violent, etc.) on your laptop.
- Do not chat online or play music/videos unless given permission by your teacher.
- Leave mobile phones turned off or in silent mode in your bags/pockets unless their use is sanctioned by a teacher for a learning activity or listening to music during independent work.
- Do not post or send any message/picture/sound/video that is obscene, rude, harassing, or insulting to anyone.
- Do not attack, threaten, or intimidate another student via technology (or otherwise).
- Do not take pictures or post pictures of others without asking their permission.

No Hogging

- Do not take up bandwidth by downloading movies, music, pictures, or by playing online games not directly connected to your learning.
- Do not store music, movies, pictures, or files on the school network not connected to your learning—all personal files must be saved on an external hard drive.

No Stealing

- Do not download any illegal materials (e.g., cracked software, pirated music or movies, or any copyrighted materials) or intellectual property that was not purchased by you or that you do not have the rights to use.

• Peer-to-peer file sharing is strictly prohibited and monitored by the School District of Philadelphia—these software programs can be detected by the District and they will shut off your access to the SDP Network.

• Do not plagiarize—i.e., present anybody else's work as your own; for more information see SLA's academic integrity policy.

• No spamming, hacking, hawking, or trolling.

• Do not forward or send any content not directly associated with your learning (e.g., advertisements, games, pictures).

• Do not deliberately or negligently spread viruses, malware, or spyware.

• Do not attempt to access any areas of the school network, or other people's devices you do not have permission to visit.

• Do not run a business or seek to make profit using the school network.

Guidelines

Science Leadership Academy and the School District of Philadelphia will monitor user data and Internet access and check the contents of any electronic device brought onto the school's premises or at any official school event.

Educational use of the network and computer resources takes precedence over noneducational use, including games not related to classwork.

This statement covers (but is not limited to) the use of electronic devices owned by the school and by students that are brought onto the school's premises, or on excursions, camps, or other official school functions—including computers, laptops, digital video and music players, cameras, other recording devices, mobile phones, and organizers.

Science Leadership Academy reserves the right to ensure all student laptops have sufficient space to support learning activities. This may include the school need to delete nonessential games, music, and video files.

Laptop Audits

Audits of student laptops can be done by any staff member at any time.

Sanctions

Sanctions for violations stated above may include the following measures:

- Confiscation of the device for a defined period
- Withdrawal of privileges including online access for breaches of online policy
- Withdrawal of the right to bring or use electronic devices to Science Leadership Academy
- Blockage from the network of any and all devices downloading illegal files such as music, video, and photographs
- Community work for the Science Leadership Academy outside school hours
- Payment for cost of repairs

Serious Breaches of Rules

- All incidences will be handled on a student-by-student basis.
- Suspension or expulsion.
- Law enforcement agencies may be involved.
- Simple Finder will be installed on your computer, which limits the applications on your laptop to strictly educational use.

The laptops are the School District of Philadelphia's property. We strongly encourage that the insurance is paid for each year the laptop is in the hands of a student. That way if there is any major damage families are only liable for the $100 deductible. Any damage caused by the user starts with the $100 deductible.

Responsibility

- Keep the computer in a safe, clean place.
- Notify SLA if the user changes residence at any point during the time they possess the laptop.
- Provide SLA and Officer Byrd with a police report in the event of fire or theft of the laptop.
- Keep the laptop in a PADDED backpack.

Administration of Computers

All users will be granted the power to change the settings within the computer. That way updates to software can be made and peripherals can be hooked up to the laptop with ease. The user may not change password settings or computer name settings; these are uniform to the school and are necessary for the maintenance and upkeep of the laptop.

File Storage

No personal files should be kept on the laptop; these must be saved to an external drive—this includes all music files and photographs. SLA is not responsible for any lost files— school or personal.

A two-gigabyte storage space will be provided for students to keep all school-related files safe—ALL FILES MUST BE SAVED TO THE DROP-BOX ACCOUNT. Further instruction on doing so will be given in the technology course during the first week of school.

Students are responsible for maintaining current backups of all their own schoolwork either online through Dropbox or their own backup solution. You will be expected to turn in your work on time even in the event that your laptop fails. The Technology Team cannot recover your files.

Network—Connecting to the Internet

The entire school is covered by a high-speed wireless Internet network. All students will be able to access the Internet, as long as they follow this policy. With this connection comes a degree of risk; this policy is made to help users avoid these risks, keep our community safe, and abide by Internet laws.

E-mail

Users will have access to an e-mail account the four years they are at SLA. You may use this to communicate with parents, teachers, friends, experts, and fellow students around the globe. An e-mail address with the suffix @scienceleadership.org will be provided to all students. This address is to be used for all school-related business. Your private account should be used for all other communications. Users will have access to their other e-mail accounts during "off" times during school, like lunch and free periods.

E-mail/Chatting Etiquette

Communicating online is very much like communicating with people in person. You must be respectful of others at all times. Remember that all e-mail & M.O.O.D.L.E. messages can be read by the SLA Technology Team and the administration. Don't write anything you would not want to share with teachers and parents.

While many members of SLA, including staff members, use instant messaging and blogging software to communicate, part of the learning experience at SLA is to responsibly use these types of communication methods as part of your school day. Students need to be aware that chatting during class time when off topic is a distraction. Students asked to refrain from using or quit using chatting during class time must do so immediately.

Publishing or Uploading to the Web

In some cases your classwork will be published or students will be asked to hand in assignments that are published. Having work published means the world can see what you have uploaded. This is a great opportunity for students as well as people not directly involved with SLA; it provides you and other students a chance to share your work and have it viewed. People curious about SLA will be visiting our web portal to see what goes on daily.

Support

The SLA Technology Office is located in room 306 and staffed by our Systems Administrator Chris Alfano. In addition, SLA's Technology Coordinator is Marcie T. Hull, who can be found in room 301.

Technology Office Hours for Student Repairs

Every day after school the last half hour of first lunch and the first half hour of last lunch.

Insurance Policy

SLA's Technology Team will determine what type of repair a laptop is eligible for and be responsible for carrying out and administering the repair.

School District Insurance—In Short

We strongly encourage the purchase of insurance available though the School District of Philadelphia for student laptop computers; the cost is $75.00. • Damage caused by the user is not covered by insurance. • Physical damage to the casing caused to chargers is not covered by insurance. • Batteries are not covered by insurance. • All damage is subject to a $100.00 deductible.

F.A.Q.'s

What do I owe up front? The money for the insurance is due at the beginning of each school year. The deductible ($100.00) must be paid when damage occurs and the user brings the laptop in for a repair that is not covered by insurance. *Users will not get the laptop back until the repair bill is paid in full.* Payment plans can be set up for your convenience.

What is not covered by the insurance? Batteries that cannot keep a charge are not covered and chargers that have physical damage to the casing.

Who pays for parts that are not covered by the insurance? In the event that a battery goes bad or the charger suffers physical damage by the user, then the user or their guardian must pay in full for the parts that are broken or missing.

Who makes the decisions about what is covered under the insurance? The coverage under this policy is dictated to us by Apple. For example, Apple considers batteries and chargers to be replaceable parts, and they are therefore not covered by insurance. SLA does not have the budget to replace these items. Therefore, should there be a problem with a battery, or a problem with a charger due to physical damage, it is the student's responsibility to pay for a replacement.

Appendix C
SLA's Academic Integrity Policy

Across disciplines, we value student collaboration and expression of original ideas. The vast majority of students turn in assignments that either meet or exceed our expectations and contain no plagiarized or copied work. In an effort to honor their work, we introduce the following policy to respond to work that has been plagiarized or copied.

Definition of Plagiarism and Academic Dishonesty for This Policy: In an instructional setting, plagiarism occurs when a student uses or supplies someone else's language, ideas, or other original material without acknowledging its source. Including, but not limited to:

- Copying from the Internet or any other source (including putting work into an online translator)
- Copying from another student
- Turning in another person's work as your own
- Submitting a group project that includes plagiarized or copied work
- Supplying another student with work that is not their own

MAJOR ASSIGNMENTS

If plagiarism/copying occurs on larger assessments in a given academic year (benchmarks, large projects worth 10% of grade or more):

-1st offense: Students will automatically fail the quarter if the assignment isn't redone. Students can redo the assignment, and any redone project that meets expectations can earn up to a 50%. The redone project's grade will be mathematically factored in to determine the student's final grade for the quarter. If plagiarism/copying is caught at the very end of the quarter, student will earn an Incomplete for the quarter and will have a maximum of two weeks to redo the assignment for 50% credit. There will also be a parent meeting with advisors, teacher, and student.

-2nd offense in any class: Student will fail the course where the second plagiarism occurs for the quarter and there will be a parent meeting with advisors, teacher, student, and Mr. Lehmann.

-3rd offense in any class: Student will fail the course where the third plagiarism occurs for the year.

Group Projects: If a group project is submitted that contains plagiarized or copied work, other group members who didn't plagiarize will be penalized one full letter grade (10%) for the project, and the group member who plagiarized/copied will fall under the above consequences. If there is a concern about a group member possibly plagiarizing or not completing his or her share of a group's work, other group members should voice this concern with their teacher as early as possible, and the teacher will work with the group to come up with a solution.

MINOR ASSIGNMENTS

If plagiarism occurs on other assignments (non-benchmarks; smaller assignments), the following consequences will apply for BOTH copier and copiee:

1st offense: 0 and redo for 0 credit, meeting with advisor and alert parents.

2nd offense in same class: meet with advisor, teacher, and Mr. Lehmann.

Additional offenses in class: parents come in and meet with Mr. Lehmann, possible suspension or failure for quarter depending on frequency of offenses.

Adapted from the Council of Writing Program Administrators, http://www.wpacouncil.org

---

Student Sign-off:

I have reviewed and understand the SLA Plagiarism Policy. All work presented in upcoming projects will be my own; I will not give or receive unauthorized help on any projects during the course of this year.

Signature: _____

Date: _____

Appendix D
Inquiry Prompts by Subject Area

English

- How are we the stories we tell?
- What experiences do you or your family have "crossing boundaries"?
- What does literary criticism show us about our own world?
- What are the relationships between language, power, and identity?
- How do men and women get what they want?
- How do social, political, and religious systems affect one's abilities to express and be true to oneself?
- What is the interplay between the public and private self?
- How can we become better readers and writers?

History

- What do you think is holding our city back from being the best it could be?
- What is the history behind your own neighborhood?
- What is a revolution? What things allow revolutions to succeed? What different things cause them to fail?
- How do we decide what and whose stories to tell?
- Does change always mean progress?
- What do historical injustices and sacrifices mean for us?

Math

- How is this mathematic function used in the world?
- Geometry: Can everything be proven? How can we make rules about the geometric world around us?
- Geometry: Can we determine an unknown measure without actually measuring? Does what we measure influence how we measure?
- Pre-Calculus: What are the relationships between algebraic representations of functions and their graphical representations?
- Pre-Calculus: What do the domain and range of a function specify regarding the application of the function in the real world?
- Pre-Calculus: How can the transformations of functions be used to demonstrate links between algebra and geometry?

Science

- Bio-Chem: If you could change one of your genetic traits, what would it be, and why?
- Bio-Chem: How can I impact the world's food supply?
- Bio-Chem: How can I impact the climate?
- Bio-Chem: What is my environmental footprint? How will my consumer decisions change after studying it?
- Physics: What do you notice about how things work?
- Physics: If we changed the forces, what do we think would happen? (What would this be like on the moon?)

Foreign Language

- How do I learn a language?
- What does language show me about culture?
- Where can I go with this language? What can I do?

Visual Arts

- What makes a compelling image or piece of media?
- How can the arts serve as a vehicle for learning about community?
- What are the best presentation tools, and how can I use them?

Engineering

- What tools did you use today?
- How does form affect function?
- How do small changes affect large systems?
- What is an effective process to utilize my skills to help the world around me?

Health

- Being a physical, intellectual, social, emotional, and spiritual being, what do you value in an intimate relationship? How do you get it?

Appendix E
Frequently Used Online Resources

English

https://owl.english.purdue.edu/—The Purdue Online Writing Lab, a comprehensive site that provides guides and practice for grammar, mechanics, composition, and citation formats.

http://nfs.sparknotes.com/—No Fear Shakespeare, online versions of most of Shakespeare's plays that present the original language next to a modernized translation for comprehension support.

http://shakespeare.yippy.com/—Shakespeare Searched, a website that allows you to search for words or phrases in all of Shakespeare's plays (or filtered by play or character).

http://www.poets.org/—Academy of American Poets, containing short biographies of poets, selected poems and recordings, and collections by theme.

http://learning.blogs.nytimes.com/—A multitude of lesson plans written by teachers using *New York Times* articles as inspiration. Current events, student voice, and vocabulary and literature are all featured.

Engineering

www.eia.gov—The U.S. Energy Information Administration, providing independent statistics and analysis about energy sources.

www.chiefdelphi.com/forums/portal.php—Practical information about motors, gear ratios, and related topics.

sciencecases.lib.buffalo.edu/cs/—Collection of over 500 case studies from the National Center for Case Study Teaching in Science, designed to teach students about the scientific process.

teachers.yale.edu/units/—A database of thousands of curriculum units in the humanities and in STEM fields prepared by teachers participating in national seminars and in seminars offered by the Yale Teachers Institute. The opening descriptions can be given directly to students as a useful introduction to new topics.

www.instructables.com—Good user-generated instructions on how to build things. Videos often include discussion of the engineering that goes into the project, instead of just construction.

Health

www.cdc.gov—The Centers for Disease Control and Prevention.

History

www.pbs.org—Educational resources that provide a nice mix of primary and secondary sources, visuals, and video.

http://italianrenaissanceresources.com—An incredible resource on the Italian Renaissance, developed in cooperation with the National Gallery of Art. The website provides eight units focused on different themes from the movement. It also includes hundreds of pieces of art, an exhaustive glossary, and 42 primary-source texts.

Foreign Language (Spanish)

www.quizlet.com—Online flash card tool that both teachers and students can use to make and share quizzes. Great for vocabulary.

www.powtoon.com—Website for making animated presentations that can be voiced over in a foreign language.

http://www.cervantes.es—Spanish website for the Cervantes Institute, with a wealth of cultural resources.

http://zachary-jones.com/—A wealth of activities, readings, songs, and articles, all in Spanish.

Math

www.purplemath.com—Math tutorial website consisting of multiple text-based descriptions of topics, example problems, and step-by-step solutions.

www.khanacademy.org—Video-based website with tutors and examples for many math and science topics.

www.processing.org—Online community for computer programming.

Science

www.ecoliteracy.org/essays/ecological-principles—Resource for the basics of ecology from the Center for Ecoliteracy.

www.epa.gov—Thorough information about environmental issues from the U.S. Environmental Protection Agency.

www.nih.gov/science/education.htm—Resources for both teachers and students about health from the National Institutes of Health.

www.physicsclassroom.com—General website with accessible information, including self-quiz questions, examples, and animations.

www.phet.colorado.edu—Website from the University of Colorado Boulder with all sorts of science simulations that allow students to manipulate conditions and explore what happens.

Visual Arts

www.creativecow.net—An active forum for media professionals who post content they are working on. Everyone is extremely helpful, and it is free.

search.creativecommons.org—The source for fair use/free copyright licenses. Unless students are producing everything themselves, they should use professional media that pay tribute to artists willing to share their work.

Appendix F
Sample Template for a Group Contract

GROUP CONTRACT TEMPLATE

TEAM NAME:

Group Member Name	Contact Information (Phone, Facebook, Twitter, E-mail)	Strengths (Personal and Academic)	Areas for Growth (Personal and Academic)

Link to Group Google Doc:

Team Roles:

Team Liaison—interacts with the teachers on behalf of the team

Team Secretary—makes sure all team documentation is in order, including calendar, Google Doc

Team Arbitrator—monitors adherence to team rules using the contract; issues warnings

Team Monitor—keeps track of project calendar and deadlines; checks assignments against the rubric; proofreads documents

Team Goals:

Use this space to describe the team's expected outcomes for this project. This should be updated regularly directly in this document and should be SMART (Specific, Measurable, Attainable, Relevant, and Time-bound).

Team Rules:

Please type additional team rules after the following three required rules. They should be based on your group's strengths and areas for growth.

1. Each team member must fulfill his or her individual duties every day.
2. Each team member must complete homework assignments as assigned.
3. A team member who will be absent must contact teammates *before* the beginning of class *and* make arrangements to compensate for the absence. Absence does not eliminate the team member's responsibilities.

Steps for Firing a Group Member:

Please type the steps for firing a group member here. The two steps below are required. Any additional steps are up to your team, pending teacher approval.

- Meeting with teacher and team
- Team member fired

Team Member Agreement:

Group member name (Pick a fun color!)	Your words about why you think this contract is going to work for you:

Appendix G
Prompts for Reflection

Prompts Related to the Individual Student

- What did you like about this project, and why?
- What did you dislike, and why?
- What did you feel successful at in this project/activity? Why?
- What did you struggle with in this project/activity? Why do you think that was?
- What parts of your project are you proud of? Why?
- What were the highlights of your project?
- How did your thinking about _____ change during this unit?
- What do you understand now that you didn't before?
- What have you done to improve your understanding of this concept?
- What was a challenge?
- How did you overcome the challenge (or challenges)?
- What is your favorite thing that you learned from this project/unit/activity?
- What are a few things you would change if you did the project/activity again?
- What connections can you make from the project/activity to your everyday life?

• What advice would you give to yourself if you were starting this project over?
• What advice would you give future students who will be doing this project?
• What would you have done with more time on this project?
• What did you learn about yourself in the process?
• What gets in the way of you being your best possible version of yourself?
• What kept you from accomplishing your goals? [Referring to the daily goals that students set for individual projects]

Prompts Related to the Process and the Group

• What is one thing you learned about project management during this project?
• Why was this group better because you were in it?
• What did your group do well?
• Where did you see room for improvement for your group?

Prompts to Guide Teacher Planning

• Which portion of the directions for this assignment would you rewrite?
• What improvements would you suggest I implement if I assign this project again next year?
• What about this type of learning works for you?
• How could I support you better as your teacher?

Appendix H
Standards by Discipline

Mathematics

There are several universal standards:

Computation and Operations: Students can perform computational and algebraic operations to the appropriate level of course.

Visual: Students can visually represent mathematical situations through graphs and diagrams.

Verbal and written communication skills: Students can clearly communicate mathematical problem solving process.

Problem solving: Students can choose and apply various problem-solving strategies to model and solve a wide variety of problems.

Plus one umbrella standard that changes by course:

Course-specific Standard: Students can apply course-specific concepts to a variety of problem situations.

Each course has standards representing course-specific concepts, which are too numerous to be printed in this appendix.

History

The standards for history courses are divided into five categories: **Sources, Research, Perspective, Discussion and Content.** Each course has a description that reflects expectations for the standard at that grade level.

Grade 12: American Government

Sources: Student can analyze a variety of primary source documents and visual representations of information.

Research: Student can independently locate a variety of sources to effectively incorporate into research-based projects.

Perspective: Student can express the impact of perspective/bias in evaluating political systems.

Discussion: In daily class activities, student can represent their ideas (in class discussion, online forums, small group, etc.) on issues relating to political theory using sources to back up their contentions.

Content: Student can evaluate connections between the modern world and the basic elements of political theory.

Grade 12: Political Theory

Sources: Student can analyze a variety of primary source documents and visual representations of information.

Research: Student can independently locate a variety of sources to effectively incorporate into research-based projects.

Perspective: Student can express the impact of perspective/bias in evaluating political systems.

Discussion: In daily class activities, student can represent their ideas (in class discussion, online forums, small group, etc.) on issues relating to political theory using sources to back up their contentions.

Content: Student can evaluate connections between the modern world and the basic elements of political theory.

Grade 11 - American History

Sources: Student can analyze a variety of primary source documents and visual representations of information.

Research: Student can independently locate a variety of sources to effectively incorporate into research-based projects.

Perspective: Student can express the impact of perspective/bias in history.

Discussion: In daily class activities, student can represent their ideas (in class discussion, online forums, small group, etc.) on history using sources to back up their contentions.

Content: Student can evaluate connections between the modern world and American History.

Grade 10: World History

Sources: Student can interpret and analyze a variety of primary source documents and utilize them in their work.

Research: Student can construct independent research-based projects.

Perspective: Student can begin to express the impact of perspective/ bias in history.

Discussion: In daily class activities, student can represent their ideas (all class discussion, online forums, small group, etc.) on history using sources to back up their contentions.

Content: Student uses the class content as a medium to build understandings and make connections between both various systems and the past and present.

Grade 9 - African-American History

Sources: Student can analyze a variety of source documents including visual representations of information.

Research: Student is making progress in producing independent research-based projects.

Perspective: Student seeks to understand and fairly present the ideas of others, even when they disagree with the point(s) being made.

Discussion: Student consistently presents his/her own idea(s) in a constructive and useful manner.

Content: Student uses the content of the class to explore and expand their understanding of the world.

English

The English standards are divided into six categories: **reading, research, thesis, grammar and mechanics, written expression, and speaking.** Each course has a description that reflects expectations for the standard at that grade level.

Grade 9: English 1

Reading: Comprehends a passage from an on-level text and masters strategies for deeper understanding and analysis.

Research: Looks at a source and identifies relevant material.

Thesis: Creates unique, insightful, and debatable thesis statement based on given topic and questions.

Grammar & Mechanics: Demonstrates a developing proficiency of the conventions of standard English capitalization, punctuation, grammar, and usage.

Written Expression: Develops a sense of voice and style.

Speaking: Communicates ideas and engages listeners effectively.

Grade 10:

Reading: Comprehends a passage from an on-level text and masters strategies for deeper understanding and analysis.

Research: Evaluates the quality of sources and identifies relevant material.

Thesis: Creates unique, insightful, and debatable thesis statement based on a given topic.

Grammar & Mechanics: Demonstrates a proficiency of the conventions of standard English capitalization, punctuation, grammar, and usage.

Written Expression: Develops a sense of voice and style across genres.

Speaking: Communicates ideas and engages listeners effectively.

Grade 11:

Reading: Comprehends a passage from an on-level text and masters strategies for deeper understanding and analysis.

Research: Uses an independent line of inquiry to evaluate the quality of sources and identify relevant material.

Thesis: Creates unique, insightful, and debatable thesis statement based on a self-selected topic.

Grammar & Mechanics: Demonstrates an advanced understanding of the conventions of standard English capitalization, punctuation, grammar, and usage.

Written Expression: Uses voice and style confidently across genres.

Speaking:
Communicates ideas and engages listeners effectively.

Grade 12:

Reading: Comprehends a passage from an on-level text and masters strategies for deeper understanding and analysis.

Research: Uses an independent line of inquiry to design and implement a complete research process.

Thesis: Crafts a formal independent research project from an original line of inquiry.

Grammar & Mechanics: Demonstrates an advanced understanding of the conventions of standard English capitalization, punctuation, grammar, and usage.

Written Expression: Uses and blends voice and style confidently across genres.

Speaking: Communicates ideas and engages listeners effectively.

Sciences

Science standards are unique to each content area, and are tethered to the five core values of the school.

9th Grade Biochemistry:

Inquiry: Student can collaboratively identify a question, and design and perform an experiment to answer that question.

Research: Student can distinguish between different research methods, scientific principles, and appropriate uses of lab equipment.

Collaboration: Student can assume a role within a group that incorporates scheduling, peer editing, and negotiation.

Presentation: Student can properly label bibliographies (with APA format), indicate measurement (metric), and organize data in spreadsheets for export to graphs.

Reflection: Student can identify patterns/trends within the research, use materials in a safe manner, and make recommendation for further research/modifications.

Grade 10 Biochemistry:

Inquiry: Student can independently identify questions, and design and perform controlled experiments to answer those questions.

Research: Student can gather and discuss meaningful data and information using multiple sources of information.

Collaboration: Student can self-design roles to contribute to the group and acknowledge people with whom they have collaborated.

Presentation: Student can effectively present his/her data and conclusions to his/her peers.

Reflection: Student can reflect upon the initial design of experiments and make suitable changes for future work.

Grades 11 and 12:

Inquiry: Student can evaluate the development of a researchable question from relevant observations.

Research: Student can gather and discuss meaningful data and information using multiple sources of information.

Collaboration: Student can provide productive feedback about the quality of collaborative work of self and peers.

Presentation: Student can communicate scientific concepts using multiple representations of a model, qualitatively and quantitatively.

Reflection: Student can suggest modifications to process for future experiments based on outcomes.

Spanish

Spanish I

Speaking

_____ Student is able to communicate by using a number of isolated words and memorized phrases using accurate pronunciation. Conversation is restricted to a few of the predictable topics necessary for survival in the target language culture. Student is able to respond to simple, direct questions or requests for information; they are able to ask a very few formulaic questions when asked to do so.

Reading

_____ Student is able to read for instructional and directional purposes standardized messages, phrases or expressions, such as some items on menus, schedules, timetables, maps, and signs.

_____ Student is able to identify an increasing number of highly contextualized words and/or phrases including cognates and borrowed words, where appropriate. Material understood rarely exceeds a single phrase at a time, and rereading may be required.

Writing

_____ Student is able to write simple fixed expressions and limited memorized material.

_____ Student is able to supply information on simple forms and documents. Can write names, numbers, dates, own nationality, and other simple autobiographical information as well as some short phrases and simple lists.

Listening

_____ Student is able to understand some words and phrases from simple questions, statements, high-frequency commands about topics that refer to basic personal information.

Cultural Competence

_____ Student is able to distinguish formal from informal situations.

_____ Student is able to identify differences between target language cultures and home culture.

Spanish 2
Speaking

Student is able to...

_____ communicate without the use of English in the classroom (Q2, Q4)

_____ narrate past events and actions (Q2, Q4)

_____ extensively describe clothing (Q2)

_____ talk about his/her daily routines using reflexive verbs (Q2)

_____ express his/her academic and professional goals using the complex future verb tense (Q4)

_____ ask for directions (Q2)

_____ check-in to a hotel (Q2)

_____ purchase transportation tickets (Q2)

_____ describe his/her personality, behavior, and favorite activities as a child (Q4)

Writing

Student is able to...

_____ describe his/her likes and dislikes in relation to any topic (Q2)

_____ narrate past events and actions (Q2)

_____ describe the color, pattern and material of clothing (Q2)

_____ describe his/her daily routines using reflexive verbs (Q2)

_____ express his/her academic and professional goals using the complex future verb tense (Q4)

_____ describe his/her personality, behavior, and favorite activities as a child (Q4)

Reading

Student is able to...

_____ navigate Spanish language travel and shopping websites (Q2)

_____ understand main ideas and supporting arguments from assigned readings (Q2, Q4)

Listening

Student is able to...

_____ understand his/her classmates without the use of English in the classroom (Q2, Q4)

_____ lengthen casual conversation by asking follow-up questions (Q2, Q4)

_____ acquire information through conversation (Q2)

_____ ask for rewording or slower speech when clarification is needed (Q2, Q4)

Cultural Competence

Student is able to...

_____ interact with respect using culturally appropriate patterns of behavior in everyday social interactions (Q2, Q4)

_____ identify some common beliefs and attitudes within Spanish-speaking culture and compare them to his/her own beliefs and attitudes (Q2, Q4)

Spanish 3
Q1/Q2
Reading

_____ Student is able to understand main ideas and some facts from level–appropriate fictional and nonfictional writing.

Writing

_____ Student can use sentences, strings of sentences, and fluid sentence-length and paragraph-length messages with frequency of errors proportionate to the complexity of the communicative task.

Speaking

_____ Student is able to effectively communicate his/her thoughts using learned expressions and vocabulary and in addition shows signs of spontaneity by independently using recombinations of learned material to convey thoughts. Pronunciation may still be strongly influenced by first language. Errors are frequent but do not impede understanding.

Listening

_____ Student is able to understand main ideas and most details of connected conversation on a variety of topics. Comprehension may be uneven due to a variety of linguistic factors (i.e. pronunciation, slang, etc.) or student is unable to drive connections between learned and new material. Dialog may include interviews, short lectures on familiar topics, and news items primarily dealing with factual information.

Cultural Competence

_____ Student is able to identify and explain the differences between culture/cultural norms in Spanish-speaking countries with his/her own culture (i.e. gender, race, and sexuality). He/she will be able to understand in depth the plight of the immigrant and the injustices evident in 3rd world countries.

Q3/Q4
Reading

_____ Student will be able to understand text with chronological sequence, information that requires minimal inference and or or to which the reader brings personal interest and/or knowledge.

Spanish 4
Speaking

_____ Student is able to handle successfully a variety of uncomplicated communicative tasks in straightforward social situations. Conversation is generally limited to those predictable and concrete exchanges necessary for survival in the target culture.

_____ Student is able to respond to questions or requests for simple information to satisfy basic needs.

_____ Student is able to use circumlocution to communicate messages.

Reading

_____ Student is able to read consistently with full understanding simple connected texts dealing with basic personal and social needs about which the reader has personal interest and/or knowledge.

Writing

_____ Student is able to write simple letters, brief synopses and paraphrases, summaries of biographical data, work and school experience. Student is able to respond in writing to personal questions.

_____ Student is able to describe and narrate in paragraphs.

Cultural Competence

_____ Student is able to compare and contrast events of historical significance and current affairs. Student is able to identify connections between target language cultures and home culture.

Spanish 5
Speaking

Student is able to...

_____ communicate and defend his/her opinions in guided whole-class discussion.

_____ relate personal experiences.

_____ discuss unfamiliar topics.

Reading

Student is able to...

_____ analyze the role of personal assumptions and cultural beliefs in the interpretation of texts.

Writing

Student is able to...

_____ produce cohesive texts composed of multiple paragraphs.

Cultural Competence

Student is able to...

_____ relate texts to products and perspectives found in a variety of media.

Art
9 - 12th

_____ Students can recognize elements, color • form/shape • line • space • texture • value

_____ Students can recognize principals, balance • contrast • emphasis/focal point • movement/rhythm • proportion/scale • repetition • unity/harmony

_____ Students can recognize, know, use, and demonstrate a variety of appropriate arts elements and principles to produce, review, and revise original works in the arts.

(• paint • draw • craft • sculpt • print • design for environment, communication, multi-media)

_____ Students can integrate and apply advanced vocabulary to the arts forms.

_____ Student can delineate a unifying theme through the production of a work of art that reflects skills in media processes and techniques.

_____ Students can analyze works of art influenced by experiences or historical and cultural events through production, performance, or exhibition.

_____ Students can incorporate the effective and safe use of materials, equipment, and tools into the production of works in the arts.

(• Evaluate the use and applications of materials. • Evaluate issues of cleanliness related to the arts. • Evaluate the use and applications of mechanical/electrical equipment.

• Evaluate differences among selected physical space/environment. • Evaluate the use and apply safe methods for storing materials in the arts.)

_____ Students can distinguish among a variety of regional arts events and resources and analyze methods of selection and admission.

_____ Students can analyze and evaluate the use of traditional and contemporary technologies for exhibiting works in the arts or the works of others.

• Analyze traditional technologies (e.g., acid printing, etching methods). • Analyze contemporary technologies (e.g., virtual reality design, instrument enhancements, photographic tools, web graphics).

_____ Students can analyze and evaluate the use of traditional and contemporary technologies in furthering knowledge and understanding in the arts.

12th

_____ Students can identify, explain and analyze philosophical beliefs as they relate to works in the arts (e.g., classical architecture, rock music).

_____ Students can explain the historical, cultural, and social context of an individual work in the arts.

_____ Students can relate works in the arts chronologically to historical events (e.g., 10,000 B.C. to present).

_____ Students can relate works in the arts to varying styles and genre and to the periods in which they were created (e.g., Bronze Age, Ming Dynasty, Renaissance, Classical, Modern, Post-Modern, Contemporary, Futuristic, others).

_____ Students can analyze a work of art from its historical and cultural perspective.

_____ Students can analyze how historical events and culture impact forms, techniques, and purposes of works in the arts.

_____ Students can know and apply appropriate vocabulary used between social studies and the arts and humanities.

_____ Students can relate works in the arts to geographic regions: • Africa • Asia • Australia • Central America • Europe • North America • South America

_____ Students can identify, describe, and analyze the work of Pennsylvania Artists in visual arts.

_____ Students can identify, explain, and analyze traditions as they relate to works in the arts.

_____ Students can identify, explain, and analyze common themes, forms, and techniques from works in the arts.

TECHNOLOGY
9-12th

1.	**Creativity and Innovation**	
	Students demonstrate creative thinking, construct knowledge, and develop innovative products and processes using technology. Students:	
	a.	apply existing knowledge to generate new ideas, products, or processes.
	b.	create original works as a means of personal or group expression.
	c.	use models and simulations to explore complex systems and issues.
	d.	identify trends and forecast possibilities.
2.	**Communication and Collaboration**	
	Students use digital media and environments to communicate and work collaboratively, including at a distance, to support individual learning and contribute to the learning of others. Students:	
	a.	interact, collaborate, and publish with peers, experts, or others employing a variety of digital environments and media.
	b.	communicate information and ideas effectively to multiple audiences using a variety of media and formats.
	c.	develop cultural understanding and global awareness by engaging with learners of other cultures.
	d.	contribute to project teams to produce original works or solve problems.
3.	**Research and Information Fluency**	
	Students apply digital tools to gather, evaluate, and use information. Students:	
	a.	plan strategies to guide inquiry.
	b.	locate, organize, analyze, evaluate, synthesize, and ethically use information from a variety of sources and media.
	c.	evaluate and select information sources and digital tools based on the appropriateness to specific tasks.
	d.	process data and report results.

4.	Critical Thinking, Problem Solving, and Decision Making	
	Students use critical thinking skills to plan and conduct research, manage projects, solve problems, and make informed decisions using appropriate digital tools and resources. Students:	
	a.	identify and define authentic problems and significant questions for investigation.
	b.	plan and manage activities to develop a solution or complete a project.
	c.	collect and analyze data to identify solutions and/or make informed decisions.
	d.	use multiple processes and diverse perspectives to explore alternative solutions.
5.	Digital Citizenship	
	Students understand human, cultural, and societal issues related to technology and practice legal and ethical behavior. Students:	
	a.	advocate and practice safe, legal, and responsible use of information and technology.
	b.	exhibit a positive attitude toward using technology that supports collaboration, learning, and productivity.
	c.	demonstrate personal responsibility for lifelong learning.
	d.	exhibit leadership for digital citizenship.
6.	Technology Operations and Concepts	
	Students demonstrate a sound understanding of technology concepts, systems, and operations. Students:	
	a.	understand and use technology systems.
	b.	select and use applications effectively and productively.
	c.	troubleshoot systems and applications.
	d.	transfer current knowledge to learning of new technologies.

References

Block, J. (2014, February 12). "Nurturing Collaboration: 5 Strategies." *Edutopia.* Available: http://www.edutopia.org/blog/nurturing-collaboration-5-strategies-joshua-block

Chen, M. (2010). *Education nation: Six leading edges of innovation in our schools.* San Francisco: Jossey-Bass.

Dewey, J. (1916). *Democracy and education.* New York: Macmillan.

Dweck. C. (2007). *Mindset.* New York: Ballantine.

Kravets, David. (2010, October 12). "School District Pays $610,000 to settle Webcam Spying Lawsuits." *Wired Magazine.* Available: http://www.wired.com/2010/10/webcam-spy-settlement/

Madden, M., Lenhart, A., Duggan, M., Cortesi, S., & Gasser, U. (2013, March 13). *Teens and technology 2013.* Pew Research Center and the Berkman Center for Internet & Society at Harvard University. Available: http://www.pewinternet.org/files/old-media//Files/Reports/2013/PIP_TeensandTechnology2013.pdf.

Purcell, K., Heaps, A., Buchanan, J., & Friedrich, M. (2013, February 28). "How Teachers are Using Technology at Home and in Their Classrooms." Pew Research Internet Project. Available: http://www.pewinternet.org/2013/02/28/how-teachers-are-using-technology-at-home-and-in-their-classrooms/

Richardson, W. (2012). *Why school?* TED Conferences.

Wiggins, G., & McTighe, J. (2013). *Essential questions: Opening doors to student understanding.* Alexandria, VA: ASCD.

Index

About the Author

Larissa Pahomov teaches students English and Journalism at the Science Leadership Academy in Philadelphia, an inquiry-driven, project-based, 1:1 laptop school considered to be one of the pioneers of the School 2.0 movement. Larissa has been published in NCTE's *English Journal* and is a contributor to the National Writing Project's Digital Is website. She lives in West Philadelphia with her husband.